AND THEN
THE NAZIS CAME

Painting by
Debra Kapneck

AND THEN
THE NAZIS CAME

A MEMOIR

SEYMOUR MAYER

To order additional copies of this book, contact:
Xlibris Corporation
1-888-795-4274
www.Xlibris.com
Orders@Xlibris.com
61399

CONTENTS

Preface.. 11

Chapter 1: Growing up in Bistrita... 13

Chapter 2: Years of Agony.. 45

Chapter 3: Separation.. 53

Chapter 4: Hardship in the Camps.. 61

Chapter 5: From Melk to Nowhere 84

Chapter 6: Ebensee 87

Chapter 7: Liberation 92

Chapter 8: Going Home... 101

Chapter 9: Going to America 119

Postscript.. 141

Acknowledgments

This book was not planned, it accumulated out of painful memories and haphazardly written notes. I avoided the subject, I never thought anything would come of it until I met Debra Kapneck, a dear friend who inspired and encouraged me to tell my story in book form.

First and foremost my deepest appreciation to my aunt and uncle Rose and Sam Hirsch whose love and caring and tireless effort made it possible for me to come to America. If there is a Heaven I'm sure they occupy a place of honor among the Saints.

A special thanks to my wife Roslyn, Roger Kohn, and Mark Toll without whose editing and proofread this would still be a work in progress.

A special thanks to William V. McDermott, M.D. for his dedication to healing and saving human life during World War II in liberated Ebensee concentration camp in Austria. With his book "A Surgeon In Combat" he validates the events of that period as no one has done before.

To the memory of
My mother and father,
Brother and sister,
My saintly grandmother,
To all my friends,
And to all my cousins, aunts and uncles
Who met their death at the hands of the Nazis.

Preface

For many years I rarely told anyone about my experiences in the Nazi concentration camps, I assumed that most people knew what happened during the war in Europe. It made no sense for me to tell a story which people were familiar with. Frankly I did not want to make others uncomfortable.

As the lone survivor of my immediate family, I cannot live out my years without telling my story and leave behind a map of my modest roots and early life. These pages will inform the reader about a colossal human tragedy that occurred in the not so distant past. This book was not planned; it accumulated out of fragmented and painful memories. At my age I hadn't much time to contemplate about it.

And Then the Nazi Came Is a personal account about my family and my generation. We lived in this peaceful town in Eastern Transylvania where the most serious challenges were settled on the soccer field. The expansion of Nazi Germany's influence in Hungary and Romania, of which many know so little, drastically changed all that. By early summer of 1944, at the age of 18, I became a slave laborer in concentration camps in Austria. These camps were not the large death camps about which so much has already been written. These were small by comparison, but the starvation, tortures and cruelties were an every day event. These small satellite camps of Mauthausen were the killing fields in Austria about which so little is known.

For over five decades historians, philosophers, religious and secular individuals have written countless works about the Holocaust. The more I listened and read, the more I became convinced that it is important I tell my story. I would like the reader to know what it was like to be enslaved at a young age for no other reason than having been born Jewish, and all the violence that was unleashed against my family and my generation.

Chapter 1

GROWING UP IN BISTRITA

My grandfather Abraham Mayer was a sharecropper. To sustain his family he grew corn on land that belonged to a Baron. After paying with crops for the use of the land there was not much left to feed his family. Since most of the land belonged to the nobility of that period, my grandfather was not poorer then most who survived by raising crops. Their main diet was mamaliga, a thick paste cooked from cornmeal and water, garnished with goat cheese, or eaten from a bowl with milk. When baked in the oven to a hard substance, it was like bread and could be cut into slices with a knife. The longer the mamaliga was baked the firmer it got; then it was called malai. For Sabbath meals, they were fortunate if they had a chicken, a home baked chalah and a cup of kosher wine to sanctify the Sabbath with the Kiddush (prayer); kosher wine for festive use only. Vegetables and cereals were also part of their diet. Fruits and nuts were in abundance.

My father, Jacob Mayer, was born into this poor family; he had five sisters, he was next to the youngest. His family lived in Nagy-Ilonda, (Ileanda in Romanian) a small village in the Jibou area of Transylvania. In 1888, the year my father was born, Transylvania was part of Austria—Hungary.

All summer my father and his siblings walked barefoot. Shoes had to last; they wore them only in cold weather and on holidays. They had no electricity no plumbing, water had to be jugged from a distant well, they were no worse off than most who survived working on a Noble's land.

I remember a story my father once told us. One year my grandfather went to the general store to buy corn seeds for planting.

The store merchant asked about his success or failure of the previous harvest. Honest Mayer, as the village people used to call him, told in great detail about his last year's poor harvest. The news spread quickly. His line of credit dropped so badly that he had a very hard time managing his affairs that year. My grandfather learned a very useful lesson; from then on his remarks about his crops were always optimistic.

My father and his sisters worked in the field. From planting to harvest time they helped their father till the soil. This was not unusual, family members at any age did work in the fields.

At the age of thirteen shortly after his Bar Mitzvah, my father left home as other young boys from poor families had done. For about a year he studied at a Yeshiva in Tusnad. The students at the yeshiva, mostly from poor families, were supported by the community. Lodging and meals were provided by different families. Breakfast and supper was usually simple, mamaliga with milk, or milk with bread. The midday meal was the main meal. Every day of the week he went to a different household that was kind and generous to invite him. That idea was called 'Days'. Yeshiva boys had to secure a patron, a family, which would provide a midday meal for each day of the week. The Sabbath meals he enjoyed most; to sit at the table, get to know the host family, talk about the events of the week and discuss portions of the Torah with the master of the house. My father valued his religious education, but he soon realized that to study at the Yeshiva was a luxury he could not afford.

In his studies he had learned that some of the wisest teachers and Rabbis also had manual skills in a variety of trades and crafts. To learn a craft my father left for Budapest. There he was fortunate to find work as an apprentice to a shoe designer and pattern maker.

He applied himself and became gainfully employed by the Mautner cipo-gjar (Mautner shoe factory) of Budapest. He often talked about his early years there. In retrospect I admired his courage and tenacity to get up and leave, interrupt his Talmudic studies, leave the old in search of the new. To live and grow old in a small village, as many have, was not a future he wanted for himself.

The early 1900's were years when able-bodied man and women were attracted to Budapest, to the opportunities offered there in the beautiful capitol of Hungary. By earning decent wages he could provide for himself and send some money home to his parents to Nagy-Ilonda. In a sharecroppers household life was hard, my father's siblings were all girls.

Buda was the older section of the city, it was known for the many crafts that were practiced there. Buda was also known my father told us, for hot springs and mineral baths. My father often spoke about the beautiful landscapes, hills and gardens surrounding the city; planting trees, grape vines and tending vegetable gardens must have been something he learned to love in his early life in Buda. Having come from a small village, at first he was intimidated by the large and beautiful city of Budapest. Then for the first time he became financially independent, could support himself and send some money home.

He then met and married a school teacher with whom he had a little girl named Rozsika. They lived happily in Buda on the other side of the architecturally famous "Chain Bridge". That is about all I remember, since not much was talked about in our home of that period of my fathers life in Budapest.

In 1914, when the First World War began, my father was drafted into the Austro-Hungarian army. During the war he served on several fronts, had a few shrapnel wounds that were not life threatening. Once in Serbia, on a foot patrol through a plum orchard, a Serb civilian jumped down on him from a tree and attempted to plant a knife in his back. Fortunately the knife went into his backpack. I also remember another anecdote about a very hot day when my father and his cavalry unit were riding through a market place of another town in Serbia. To quench his thirst he bought a drink from a street vendor, the drink nearly knocked him off his horse. He assumed the drink would be refreshingly cold and not very hot.

My father survived four years of war without a serious injury but not his wife. During the influenza epidemic of 1917-1918 when millions died all over Europe, she also lost her life. In the last year of the war my father had advanced to corporal and was stationed in the city of Hermanstadt (Sibiu in Romanian) Transylvania.

At the end of the war, the Austro-Hungarian Empire was broken up. Many of the regions that were part of the empire became independent states. Transylvania became part of Romania. My father chose to return to his parents in Transylvania and took his little girl with him.

My mother's family lived in Prizlop, also a small village, not a great distance from where my father came. My mother had a brother Chaim and an older sister Rozsi. During the war my grandmother feared for her daughters' safety. They were young women of marrying age, and the soldiers were not on their best behavior.

Because of that, my grandmother moved her family to the city of Besztercze.

I don't know how my parents met. My mother was eight years younger than my father. To his new marriage he brought his 7-year-old little girl, Rozsika. In 1921, my mother's sister married, then after a few months emigrated to the United States.

When I was born my half sister Rozsika was 13-years-old. My older sister Rifka was five, and my brother Bumi was 3. My half sister Rozsika was a very pretty and lively girl. She had a pleasant voice and loved to sing. She taught us many games; we learned much from her. I wish I could remember more about those early years of my childhood. The events that followed shaped our lives. To a large degree many issues are still very troubling to me, family issues that have not been resolved to this day.

At the age of 18 my half sister Rozsika committed the then unforgivable deed. She eloped and married a man outside our faith. In those days, that was the worst that could happen to a Jewish family.

It was like an indelible stain. By the standards of that period, for my mother that irresponsible behavior against custom was impossible to accept. As for my father having lived in Budapest he had a more modern view, he was less judgmental and accepted his daughters wishes. The harmony that had existed in our family was shattered. My mother and father never stopped blaming each other. From then on, our lives were never to be the same again. In the Jewish community we were looked upon with suspicion and mistrust. With hindsight we did not deserve to be treated that way. At home we were discouraged from talking about her; some time after, we even stopped mentioning her name. I was too young to understand what was happening. I accepted and followed my mother's wishes.

My half sister had two boys, Ernest and Mihai. Although they lived in a small town about 20 kilometers from Bistrita, I had no opportunity to see them except on one occasion when my father asked me to go with him: He had something to show me he said, and it would be a big surprise for me. It was on a Tuesday; every Tuesday was our town's weekly big market day. People came from villages near and far; they brought all kinds of farm produce for sale, then shopped the stores for goods to take home. To my surprise I was taken to see my sister whom I had not seen since she left home, and my little nephews who were as bewildered as I was at the meeting. After our short visit I had to promise my father to keep this as our secret. I was to tell no one about our meeting. It was like an oath I kept my promise. Since Rozsika was part of my father's former life, my mother and father could not equally share in the loss. They both suffered much, but in different ways. Years later I had the sense that my father was more forgiving than my mother.

Bistrita, Transylvania. The Romanians called it Bistrita, the Hungarians Besztercze, and the Saxons called it Bistritz. Speaking Yiddish or German we called the city by its German name.

In the 13th century, Bistritz was already an important commercial settlement. For fear of the Tartars, the Huns and other Barbarians who for centuries swept across the Carpathian Mountains, looting, burning homes and fields, and terrorizing the peasants of the region, the town's people built a fortress wall that surrounded the city. Taking positions behind the fortress wall the defenders could stop the attacking invaders. With the ability to defend themselves, the population of the city grew and prospered. In a few places, sections of the original fortress wall still stand.

In the 15Th century, a large Gothic Cathedral with a tower approximately 75 meters high was built in the center of the city. In years to come the tower served as an early warning system, the approaching enemy could be seen from afar. The defenders could gain precious time by taking defensive positions inside the fortress.

The high tower still serves the city well. The huge clock with Roman numerals with faces on all four sides can be seen from a great distance, and is well illuminated at night. Below the clock a narrow balcony wraps around the tower. To the balcony and the room where the watchman was on duty, I once climbed the many hundreds of spiraling steps. The room was spacious and comfortable; there may have been two persons taking turns on duty. It was not easy to be a watchman in that tower. To get up there, one had to climb many arduous spiraling stone steps.

In case of fire anywhere from any direction, the guard would alert the city by pulling the rope of an ominous sounding bell, then place a red lantern in the direction of the fire. The volunteer Firefighters rode their bicycles to the fire station and then, with horse drawn extinguishing equipment, they rushed in the direction the red lantern pointed. By day they rode in the direction of the billowing smoke. Although primitive by today's standards the city was self sufficient in many ways; electricity was supplied by its own waterfall generated power station.

We had an efficient post office with mail delivery service, well paved streets and roads, churches of every denomination, a primary synagogue, a school system from elementary to upper high school, competent artisans, artisans in every field and stores with goods of many varieties. There was a single rail line from Cluj through Bistrita to the Borgos and beyond to the other side of the Carpathian Mountains. The telephone system was in its infancy; there were very few private telephone lines. Two taxis were the only motorcars. Other transportation was by horse drawn carriages and bicycles. Both my father and my brother had their own bicycles; occasionally my brother would let me ride his. The city was lively with pedestrians; one could walk from one end to the other in any direction in about an hour.

The population of Bistrita was divided among Romanians, Hungarians, Saxons, Jews and Gypsies. The mixed population lived reasonably well together. Aside from the ages-old anti-Semitism, the Jewish population actively participated in the life and culture of the city. The national government was a Democratic Monarchy ruled by King Carol II.

The Romanian language is related to other romance languages. Very close to Italian and French, its origin goes back to the period when the Roman Emperor Trajan settled the area then called Dacia. In high school, French was taught as a second language.

The Hungarians rarely spoke Romanian; neither did the Saxons, who spoke a Saxonian German. Most of the Romanians were in agriculture and forestry. In high school my classmates were sons of Romanian farmers and military officers, I got along well with them. We were all eager to learn.

The Romanian national dress was colorful and probably still is the same. Over their trousers the men wore long heavy white linen shirts with wide full-length sleeves colorfully embroidered. At the waist they wore wide leather belts, also embroidered with intricate patterns.

For footwear they had the Opinca, a shaped form of rawhide leather, pulled up at the toe and held on with a rawhide lace crisscrossing over the instep of the foot, then several more times around the ankle and over the calf of the leg. To enhance attraction, little jingling bells were sometimes attached to the straps around the calves. They wore lambs' fur hats called Caciulas. The Romanian women's national dress was equally beautiful, hand embroidered white linen dresses with colorful long aprons, front and back.

There were distinct cultural differences between the Romanians and the Hungarians. In 1940 the Hungarians of Transylvania followed whatever Budapest offered in fashion, music and film. The film idols were Yavor Pal, Bela Lugosi, the Gabor sisters and others of that period. Years later the Gabor sisters went to America, and Bela Lugosi also became a leading actor in an early film as Count Dracula. The Hungarian language is difficult to learn for speakers of German or Romanian.

The Saxons are Lutherans. They were good artisans, they owned the best businesses, and lived in the nicest homes; the Gothic Cathedral in the center of the

17

city was theirs. They spoke regular German with a Saxonian dialect. Those in the rural areas outside the city were good farmers. Their produce was superior and sought after in the market place.

Our family doctor was a Saxon who rode a bicycle to make house calls. He was a good doctor my father liked him, we were glad to have him as our family doctor. Our dentist was Dr. Teichman. My mother took me to the dentist often; my oral health was not good. I was ten years old when I got my first toothbrush. Twice a year I had tonsillitis, each time I stayed home from school for a few days. To speed up my recovery my father used to paint my tonsils with a goose feather dipped in kerosene. It usually worked, my throat became anesthetized and I could swallow without pain. Yes, compared to today's standards. In many ways we lived primitive lives.

The Jewish population of Bistrita lived and worked side by side with their non Jewish neighbors. The Beitler gasse (street) was primarily Jewish.

On the street where we lived, there were only three Jewish families. Our neighbors were both Saxons and Hungarians. Jews worked in the same trades and occupations as the others. A fair number were teachers and doctors. We had an accredited Jewish elementary school but my father chose to enroll us in the state run elementary and high schools. He did not want us to live in a self-imposed separation of any kind. We lived in friendly relations with our neighbors.

Throughout the political history of the region, Transylvania's Hungarians and Romanians, at one time or another, considered the other as minority. Before the First World War, Transylvania was part of Hungary, after the war the region became part of Romania.

The discontent and friction between the Romanians and the Hungarians had been ongoing for centuries. In 1940, the northern half of Transylvania was ceded to Hungary. Since the end of World War II all of Transylvania is again under Romanian rule.

Our house was built on a street lined with Linden trees. When the trees were in full bloom, the fragrance was a delight. Our house had two street fronts. The main entrance was on Regina Maria Street, number 76.

The house extended all the way to the other parallel street with an entrance on Principesa Elizabeta number 35. Our living quarters were on one side of the length of the property; on the other side we had a small rose garden surrounded by fruit trees. My father planted the rose garden and the fruit trees. It was not a large garden. He took great pride in planting and caring for the rose trees: They were not rose bushes. In the fall before the snow and cold weather arrived he carefully bent the fragile trunks so he could bury the crowns under hay mixed with manure from the barn. The rose trees in the middle, and the fruit trees around the edge of the garden. We had two summer apple trees, one apricot and one pear tree.

The fruit trees bore fruit for three years before we were deported. Between the rose garden and the hay shed was the barn with a cow for milk, next, two large sheds for firewood. Towards the Elizabeta Street, in the middle of the yard stood an old apple tree that gave us apples every year. The apples used to fall down before they had a chance to ripen, they were not very sweet but the worms liked them. When I bit into an apple and found a worm, I felt I had invaded the worm's habitat. Along our neighbor's high brick wall my father planted a number of grape vines with trellises to climb and cling to. In a couple of seasons the wall was covered with bunches of dark red sweet grapes ready for picking.

My father loved to grow things. He planted the rose garden and the fruit trees. Not far from our home, he also rented a plot of bare ground where he grew a variety of vegetables. I enjoyed working with him in the garden. I loved going to the garden and pick a basketful of ripe tomatoes, cucumbers, green peppers and string beans. Our home grown vegetables tasted great; better than those from the market. On the Regina Maria Street, between the linden trees, the soil was very rich and black. In summer after a rain, many white button mushrooms sprung from the ground. My father seldom missed a chance to pick some; roasted lightly on hot coals with a little salt, the mushrooms were delicious. I believe it was then that I developed a taste for mushrooms.

On hot summer days I could always depend on going to the canal to cool off. My father used to seat me on the bicycle bar and off we went for a swim in the canal. On those occasions I also learned how to eat fish, it was easy to catch a few. After we cooled off, he made a small fire from dry twigs we gathered along the bank of the canal, then wrapped two fish in newspaper and placed them on the fire. When the paper had burned off, the fish was also done. After we peeled the charred paper off, the white meat was exposed and ready to eat. Just thinking about it I can still taste that sweet fish flavor.

When I was about ten years old, my mother arranged for me to visit with her cousins for a few days, two sisters who lived in Beclean; their mother had died recently and they wanted company. Why I was chosen for that I didn't know, maybe because my older brother and sister didn't want to go.

On a Tuesday in July, after the market day, I went by ox cart about 20 km. to Beclean. By the time we arrived I was sore all over; I felt every rut in the road. It had not rained for a while. It was very hot. Whenever a horse drawn carriage passed us, a cloud of dust enveloped us. We finally arrived and my mother's cousins were waiting for me. I don't remember the younger sister's name, but Matilda the older, had been married for a few years, then something went wrong. Her husband had to be institutionalized in a mental hospital. Whenever the subject was brought up in our home, it was always whispered about, as if anyone had been listening. It's strange how a story like that reserved space in my memory.

The cousins were nice to me. They lived in a small house on a side street not far from the center of town. A Hungarian Baron named Betlehen once owned the whole town it was more like a large village; the town was named after him. The cousins told me about the Baron's mansion with 40 rooms. Sometime in the distant past, the mansion was occupied by the Baron and his large family. Hundreds of serfs and their families worked and lived on the land. The mansion had been unoccupied for many years. The regional government preserved it for posterity; it was kept open to visitors.

We made plans to go there the next day. After supper they showed me my room. The sisters shared one room; they gave me the other.

The walls were white washed and clean, the kitchen had a compacted dirt floor; it was the coolest room in the house. I was tired and went to bed early looking forward to tomorrow.

I hardly slept all night. For some reason I was very restless. When daylight came through my window, I knew what the problem was, I was already home sick. I didn't know what to do. In shorts and sandals, I walked outside to look around.

I saw a bus turn into Main Street. It had a printed sign with Bistrita on it. I was so homesick nothing could stop me. I ran back to the house, told Matilda that I was going home with the bus that was leaving in a few minutes. I climbed on the bus and took a back seat.

I can't imagine what my once or twice removed cousins must have thought of me. They didn't try to talk me out from leaving; I don't remember if I paid the fare or not. In a short while I was back in Bistrita. I ran all the way home from the bus station. My mother was in the yard feeding the chickens. I was so happy to be back home I couldn't stop crying. My mother embraced me; to calm me down she gave me a bowl of wild strawberries with lots of sugar on top. I still kept crying, my tears were all over the strawberries. Whenever I see wild strawberries, I remember that moment. They were the sweetest tasting strawberries I ever had.

We had a dog named Prince, a German shepherd; he had more lives than any cat as the saying goes. He came to us as a puppy.

I remember when my father was followed home by this small, friendly animal. He came up to our kitchen door. There he stopped and would not go inside. That was a good omen for him, had he entered, my mother would have insisted that my father take him back to where he came from. I don't remember any of my friends having had pets. Dogs were plentiful in town; most were playful and friendly to passersby. After a playful afternoon if they were not caught by the dogcatchers, they usually returned home to their owners. There was a time when there were too many dogs on the streets. The city government organized a dog catcher brigade; a unit of about four to six Gypsy men, a horse drawn cart with a large wire cage. Each man had a long broom size wooden stick with a wire noose at one end. Once the dog's neck was caught in the noose, after a little struggle, the dog surrendered meekly. Usually the owners ransomed their dogs from the pound. Prince had his doghouse against the wall near the grapevines. I had no leash for him. He never strayed far away and always returned within minutes. He was well fed, ate leftovers from the table and occasionally chewed on a marrowbone that my father brought home from the kosher butcher shop. There was no such thing as store bought dog food.

There was a time when Prince was caught and my father had to pay for his release. Then Prince was caught again, and again he paid ransom to get him back. Prince was too trusting, he allowed himself to be caught. When the dog catchers passed on our street they lingered near our house just waiting for Prince to appear.

After a number of ransom payments, my father decided to get even with the dog catchers. When Prince was caught again my father followed the horse drawn cage. At a moment when the dog catchers were running after a dog, my father raised the lid of the cage and all the dogs jumped out and ran for their lives. We realized we could no longer keep him, my father found a home for Prince on a farm. I missed his occasional bark, the dog house stood empty for a long time, after Prince we never had another dog.

For cooking and heating we burned fire wood. We always had an ample supply. Since we burned only wood we consumed a lot. Split logs came cut about a meter long in size. On delivery day four to five oxcarts piled high were dumped in the middle of our yard. Then the wood cutters came with their large circular saw. The machine had an electric motor that was connected with long cables to a power line in the street. The end of the cables had hooks made of copper. To connect to the power line in the street, the men used a long wooden pole to raise the hooks one at a time. I knew to keep a distance from the cables; sometimes they were not insulated as well as they should have been. Each log was cut into 3 or 4 pieces, and then the wood choppers arrived with their axes. It took about a week for three men to finish chopping and stacking the fire wood. Most of the time the wood came directly from the forest. We burned last year's wood first, because green wood smoked a lot and didn't burn well.

I remember witnessing a near tragic accident that happened to Mendi Gruber. One morning Mendi was on his way home, playfully with his arms stretched out pretending to fly like an airplane. I was walking at a short distance in back of him.

As the distance between us shortened I could hear him humming, imitating the sound of an airplane, then suddenly I saw him, his right hand grasping the electric cable that hung from the overhead electric wires. His scream was so terrible I knew he was in serious danger. The only thing I could do was to yell for help. I ran into the open courtyard yelling for help. The Hebrew teacher from this little shull heard my call, he ran out and saw Mendi wrapped around the hanging cable. The teacher managed to free Mendi's hand by that time his hand was raw flesh from the burn. Fortunately the teacher happened to be a very muscular strong man; otherwise much worse could have resulted. I was in shock to have witnessed the accident but I was glad I was there that probably saved his life.

Mendi Gruber was my age; we went to the same elementary school. In third grade he was left behind to repeat the year; we were still friends but in school we were a year apart. He also survived the camps but did not return home to Bistrita. We were informed that after liberation he was taken to Sweden for medical treatment.

After my grandfather Mandel, on my mother's side died, my grandmother began a small bake shop business. Her apartment was one large room. At the rear was her bedroom, towards the middle was her sitting room and in front near the entrance, was the large brick oven and kitchen. On Fridays, women used to bring their chalah dough; my grandmother braided the dough into chalah and baked them in her oven. After they were baked, the oven was hot enough to cook the cholent; a meal that was left in the hot oven to cook overnight in earthenware pots. For most of the Jewish families that was the main Sabbath meal. Baking for others, my grandmother earned enough money to cover her rent and other living expenses.

I attended Hebrew school six days a week from Sunday to Friday. On the way to school I used to stop by to see my grandmother; she always had something for me, a cookie, a piece of fruit or candy. She had a way with children. Her favorite was to sit on a low stool and invite me to sit in her lap. Her wide skirt felt like sitting in a hammock.

She was a kind person I loved her everybody loved her.

My grandmother was mindful of other people's needs. Poverty was widespread, entire families without any means of support in faraway villages in the Maramures region of Transylvania. Women left their homes, their families, and went begging from town to town, eating and sleeping in homes that welcomed them. After weeks on the road, the few Lei's (Romanian currency) the nickels and dimes they saved they brought home to their families. A few such women who came to my grandmother always found a warm meal and a clean bed.

I remember a story my grandmother once told us. Many years ago when she was a young woman, she was a passenger in a horse drawn wagon going from her village to the town of Somcut. Soon as they left they were on a badly rutted road, then out of nowhere, a motor car drivers horn startled the horse and took off wildly. The driver lost the reins, her carriage turned over and my grandmother was pinned underneath the carriage. When they found her she was badly bruised, the skin on her arms and legs was scraped to the bone. She believed that her recovery from that accident was due to a miracle; she also believed that she was saved for a special purpose, to help others in need and do good things in life.

When my grandmother gave up her baking enterprise, she came to live with us. Again she had her own one room apartment with a private entrance; it was a large room with two large windows facing the yard. Her furniture was simple, the same furniture she had in her apartment on the Beitler Street. The room was rectangular; the wall that separated her room from our living quarters was a makeshift wall that was added sometime in the past. Two pieces of home art decorated her wall. On a yellowish linen cloth, framed in a scalloped border, all hand stitched in red, were two portraits facing each other: Franz Joseph, Emperor of Austria Hungary, with another popular noble of that time, with a slogan

"Mi erosen es husegen ossze tartung," We are united in loyalty and strength. The phrase in Hungarian was arching like a rainbow above their heads.

The other handmade home art was a starched piece of linen with a narrow border, in bold letters it read, "Barbatul meu numai apa bea"

(My husband drinks water only) The unframed wall decorations represented two cultures, one displaying a Romanian virtue of not drinking alcohol, the other professing loyalty to each other; the Emperor Franz Joseph and perhaps the Prussian ruler.

My grandmother could read the prayers. The prayer book was printed in Hebrew letters. When read, it was the good old Yiddish language. During the week she prepared her own meals but fasted every Monday and Thursday. She enjoyed good health, perhaps because she fasted two days a week. With her special incantations she performed old-fashioned miracles. For small ailments my grandmother was our resident doctor. When I complained of having a headache she immediately got a glass of cold water and some hot coals from the wood burning stove. While I was sitting on her lap she dropped the hot coals in the glass of water, slowly one by one. As the coals fell into the water, each made a swishing sound, and with each drop my grandmother whispered her magical words. My grandmother believed in the existence of an Evil Eye that had to be excised before it could do harm. Her magic worked most of the time.

We had a yard full of chickens; geese, a few ducks and at times we had a few turkeys also. The result was that we had lots of feathers, lots of warm feather-bedding and pillows filled with goose down feathers. Our mattresses were filled with straw and everything imaginable except feathers; every day they had to be plumped up.

On long winter nights, my grandmother organized feather-plucking parties. On a large table with a kerosene lamp in the middle, she and her companions plucked feathers for many hours into the night. They plucked chicken and goose down feathers; they were careful not to mix them. Every other evening they plucked feathers of a different bird, they drank tea and ate baked sweet pumpkins. On the surface the American pumpkin looks the same, except the Romanian did not grow so large but was as sweet as our sweet potato in America.

In the fall, when the plums famous to our region were fully ripe, we made lekvar (plum preserve). It was a yearly ritual. We made a fire in the yard; to keep the hot coals from spreading we surrounded the fire with stones. On an iron tripod, we placed a large copper kettle filled with ripe plums (the kettle was rented by the day). It took many hours to cook the plums down, from early afternoon until 2 or 3 of the next morning. To prevent the plums from sticking to the bottom of the kettle we constantly mixed the stuff with a long L shaped wood paddle. Throwing logs on the fire, watching the sparks fly in the brisk night air, taking turns with the wooden mixer, and always someone singing made the evening exciting. At the start the kettle was full to the brim, by the time the cooking was done, the kettle was about half full or less. I often wanted to stay up to the end, but about midnight I became too sleepy.

My grandmother knew old peasant songs, songs she learned when she was young. My father also used to hum a tune from an old Hungarian song; at times I heard a few words. "Akacas ut ha vegig menyek rajtad en, eszembe jut egy nyari szep regeny"—(When I walk on the acacia road, a memorable summer story comes to mind, so on and so on). The song must have meant a lot to him, I heard him hum it often. My half sister Rozsika had a pleasing voice, but she was no longer with us.

During summer months we had much free time. We played with home made games we were inventive we created them. Store bought toys or games did not exist; there were no toy stores in existence. The game of chess and dominoes were widely known and played at many levels. We played cards 21 and rummy made out of wooden blocks. A home made game called mill and the popular game of Ping-Pong. The game of Ping-Pong was widely played at different levels of skill. I loved that game, most of my friends did, we played all summer outdoors none of us had room for a Ping-Pong table indoors. The German club probably had all year round game facility but we had no membership in that club. And, of course I loved and played soccer football.

23

One day my father bought a second hand violin hoping that one of us would be interested in taking lessons. It had strings and all, it came inside a black box lined with a faded blue velvet fabric, snapped shut with brass clips. My brother was not interested; it fell on me to take violin lessons from a Gypsy musician who lived near the terra-cotta oven factory about a kilometer from our home. At first I was exited about the arrangement but I'm sorry to admit that after the first lesson I never went back. It was a winter day, it was freezing cold, by the time I arrived I was soaking wet from the icy cold rain. The experience was memorable, by the time I arrived home after the lesson; I decided not to go back.

One summer, an exceptional performer Schtrohschneider, the famous tightrope walker came to town. I remember his name, because I had never seen a more daring performance. In a circus the tightrope walker performs under the big top 20 or 30 feet high, Herr Schtrohschneider performed at a height of about 60 feet or more above ground. A cable was tied to the tower in the center of town, just below the wrapped-around balcony below the clock; from there the cable was stretched across the open space to the top of the roof of the highest building opposite the tower.

On three consecutive summer nights he performed without a safety net. Besides the usual back and forth crossings with the long balancing bar in his hands, he also carried a table, a chair and a lantern to the center of the distance. He then very carefully sat on the chair, with the lit lamp on the table in front of him. The gathered viewers were awed by the spectacle. The surroundings were completely dark except for the spot lights that illuminated the length of the cable. During the performance nobody dared make the slightest noise; people whispered to each other in disbelief. During and after the performance, contributions of coins were dropped into hats the organizers of the event passed around.

For a number of years the tight rope walker was a sensation everywhere, until we heard of an unfortunate accident.

Somewhere, after he completed his act, a few drops of rain fell on the cable and caused him to slip and fall. He survived the fall but could never perform again.

To walk on a cable or rope, from one point to another, was a challenge that many boys tried to imitate. They walked on broomsticks supported by wooden crates at each end; others walked on horizontally placed ladders. The fascination caught on, everywhere kids practiced the walk.

Sammy Einhorn lived in a house on a street near the canal that powered the turbines of the electric company. To go to the football stadium we had to cross the canal on a short wooden bridge. The wooden side rails were about waist high. On different occasions, passersby saw Sammy walk back and forth on the rails. He was cautioned numerous times and was told it was too dangerous and he might fall. When Sammy failed to come home after school one day, they knew where to look for him. He was found tangled in some tree branches at the bottom of the canal.

My aunt Esther, my father's youngest sister, was very devoted to her ailing mother; she was the only one who did not marry. After her mother (My grandmother on my father's side,) died, my aunt Esther came to live with us. By then she herself was very sick. She had fluid in her lungs and the doctors could not help her much. Our family doctor, who made house calls on a bicycle, came often, but the medications he prescribed did no good. My aunt Esther spent weeks in bed. Her condition did not improve. My grandmother did everything to make her comfortable. One day after coming home from school, I was told that my aunt Esther had died.

I heard my grandmother tell how Esther began to see the Angel of Death, how aunt Esther held on to Bobbie (we called grandmother Bobbie) and cried "Bobbie don't let him take me away, don't let the Angel of Death take me I am so afraid"

I was very young then, but still remember how frightened I was to hear how aunt Esther died. That afternoon and evening was full of mystery.

I knew of death and dying, but this was our own death, under our roof. In my town undertaking the handling and disposing of the dead had not yet been developed into an industry. The so called friendly undertaker did not exist. The Chevra Kedusha, the Jewish burial society provided the customary ritual service. Since burial took place the next day, the deceased remained in the home overnight except when the person died late in the day on a Friday; too late for same day burial, then burial was delayed till Sunday. I was not allowed to enter the room but managed to peek through a small hole in the makeshift wall. My aunt Esther covered with a white sheet was laid out on the floor, with two lit toll candles, one on each side of her head. My mother, grandmother and other women stood vigil all night. Next day she was taken to the Jewish Cemetery and buried in a plain pinewood coffin. As was the custom, before the end of the first year of her death, a rough marble headstone with aunt Esther's last and first name chiseled in Hebrew letters was dedicated to mark her grave.

Some years later my father, my brother and I went to the cemetery. The head stone was tilted to one side, the chiseled inscription was readable, the graveyard appeared neglected; toll grasses covered all the grave sites. It was not the custom to have perpetual care. On our way home from the cemetery my father told us about her, what a kind person she was, how she cared for their parents. My grandparents, her mother and father were sick for years before they died. Her sisters, my other aunts, were married; they had families of their own with their own problems. Esther had been the youngest, single and very devoted to their parents. She neglected herself, when she came to live with us she was very ill. My father kept saying, "She was too young to die, she was too young to die"

Our neighbor on the other side of the brick wall was a professional chimney sweeper; he was a Saxon and spoke German. With a spiral cable and a long thick brush at one end, he came to our house twice a year to sweep our main chimney.

Before he climbed inside to perform his task, he would wrap himself up like a mummy, covering everything except the slits of his eyes. He looked comical dressed in black, with the long rolled up cable and the huge, long black brush over his shoulder. His work was very important; without his service the wood shingled roofs would catch on fire from the sparks a dirty chimney emitted.

On the Elizabeta Street, about four houses away from our home, there was this unusual and unnoticed structure behind a toll wooden fence. In the middle of the yard there was this large deep hole, excavated for storing blocks of ice. Above ground this wide stone wall structure had an opening through which the ice was deposited in winter and retrieved in summer. During winter days and sometime for weeks, our (Bistrita) river used to freeze over. The ice was then chopped into large blocks, loaded onto oxcarts, and then hauled to the ice storage hole in the ground. At times six or more ox drawn carts lined up for their turn to unload and deposit the blocks of ice. During the summer the ice was sold and used for the iceboxes in people's homes.

My sister Rifku contracted polio before I was born. As a young child I didn't understand why she walked differently than the rest of us; she walked with a slight limp. Walking together she always held my hand, as she leaned on her weak leg she pulled and pushed my hand downward, she could not help it. Pressing down that way she found her balance. She had long wavy chestnut brown hair, brown eyes and her face radiated a special beauty. She was very sensitive and thoughtful. Because of her physical defect she was always very self-conscious and withdrew from most social activities. She chose her friends carefully. Some of her classmates were insensitive, at times some of them were cruel, they made fun of her by calling her unkind names. She loved her school studies and enjoyed reading and needle point. My mother and sister were constant companions. She corresponded with our aunt Rose in America, who had no children of her own. Our aunt wanted my sister to go to America and live with her, but Rifku would not even consider it; America was too far she chose to stay home.

Had she gone she would have been saved. In 1949 when I came to America and stayed with our aunt in Brooklyn I recognized a framed needle point on the wall. My sister Rifka had sent it about five years earlier. A small landscape, my aunt gave it to me, I still have it. Other than family portraits sent to our aunt over the years before the war, the needle point is the only thing I poses that my sister made, every stitch of it.

My brother Bumi and I were different in every way. He was very private about his interests, and almost never included me in any of his activities. At the time I was not happy about it. After school he could always be found at the bicycle shop, he loved to work with his hands. My father did not smoke cigarettes, but my brother began to smoke at an early age. He never smoked in our presence, but I had seen him smoke cigarettes with his friends in the park. One day father and I were going home and Bumi was walking toward us. Just a few steps from him, we noticed smoke coming from his wind breaker. A hole had burned through above the elastic at his waist. He'd been smoking, when he saw us coming he hid the lit cigarette under his jacket. My brother was so upset; he feared our father would punish him. On the contrary, father began to laugh, he thought it was comical the way Bumi tried to retrieve the burning cigarette from under his jacket. Bumi was tall for his age, whereas I was the second or third smallest in the line up of my class in school. I rarely had new clothes. When Bumi got a new pair of pants or a new jacket his outgrown clothes were made over to fit me. New clothes were expensive; we had to economize that way.

I remember my school days well. My elementary school, a multi level brick building on Regina Maria Street, across the street from our home. From my classroom window on the second floor I could see my mother in our yard. My mother did all the house work, cleaning, cooking, feeding the chickens and milking the cow twice a day morning and evening so that we could have fresh milk. Then came a time when the zoning board forbade domestic animals on our street such as cows but not horses.

From then on we had to buy our milk. On Tuesday mornings my mother baked bread for the week. While the bread was in the brick oven, from saved dough she could quickly bake placintas, a flat bread filled with a mixture of cheese and herbs. (Similar to the Pitas from the Middle East)

At intermission between classes, I used to run across the street to have some of that freshly baked delicacy. My classroom was large, up to thirty-five boys in a room. We had to buy our own textbooks and other school supplies. Since most could not afford new text books, we traded in books; as long as the pages were not abused too much it was easy to restore a book. Brown paper from grocery bags or shiny news print from magazines made good book covers. The teachers were strict, homework had to be completed; for unsatisfactory work one could be left behind to repeat the grade. Physical punishment by teachers in the classroom was normal and widely accepted.

After school I went to cheder (Hebrew school) every afternoon. Herr Adler my teacher was very strict. For the smallest infractions he never missed an opportunity to punish his students. With a long stick, he used to hit the open palm of both hands, not just once but twice. Had I told my parents about it, I'm sure they would have found another teacher for me: Physical punishment in Hebrew School was also widely accepted then, but not by my parents.

Before I went to High school I had another teacher at another Hebrew school, his name was Mr. Wax. I remember his apartment with his tall and lanky spouse; they had no children of their own. Mr. Wax sat at the head of the long uncovered wooden table while eight or ten boys sat on either side with open books following the teacher's instructions. Between the pages of his open book were lots of hair from his beard. He used to insert his fingers through his long beard and the loose hair fell onto the pages in front of him. I was so preoccupied watching his movements that I completely forgot to follow his instructions. If I haven't learned much from him at least I remember him for something.

Liceul "Alexandru Odobescu" my high school, about a 10 minutes walk from my home. I had great teachers who made learning exciting.

A new world opened up for me, new languages, French and Latin, ancient to modern history, with geography to support the events in their time and place. After each lecture I felt as if I had been to ancient Egypt, the Nile River and the pyramids, the Persian Empire, Mesopotamia, the Tigris and Euphrates Rivers, the beginning of civilization, the Greek Empire with Alexander the Great, who thought himself and his legions invincible, the Romans and the Ottomans whose footprints still influence the cultures of the Balkan countries, Valachia (Old Romania) and Transylvania to this day.

Our high school had a good scholastic reputation. Students came from all parts of the country; from Jasi, Craiova, Timisoara and from as far as Constanza near the Black Sea. Alexandru Odobescu was an all boys school with boarding facilities off campus.

In my class of 25 to 28 students, four were Jewish boys. Besides me, the others were Eddy Goldstein, Tibi Simon and Jeno Olbaum. These classmates were also my close friends. At the end of each semester we were given both written and oral exams. I recall one incident, I was delinquent in paying my tuition and was ejected from my algebra class. The professor had just posted four problems, each with several unknown factors, we were allowed two hours for the exam. To solve the problems we had to create correct equations, then the rest was easy. When the bursar came into the room, and called out a few names, and mine among them, we were sent home for non payment of tuition. I ran out of the school to find my father to let him know what happened. My father took his gold pocket watch with chain to the pawn shop to get the money I needed. With paper money in my hand, I ran back to school and gave the money to the bursar. When I got back to my class room I had a half-hour left to complete the test. We were seated two to a bench, the fellow to my right said "What took you so long?" intimating that most were finding the problems too difficult to solve. The professor was reading a book at his desk in front of the long classroom.

To help my classmates I noted the equations on bits of paper, rolled them into little clumps and tossed them to the back of me; with the equations they had no difficulty completing the test.

At that moment I did not realize how stupid I was to risk being caught, but when I saw how desperate some of my classmates were, I couldn't help myself.

While in high school I went to Yeshiva three times a week to study Mishna and Gemara (Bible studies). We sat at a long table with the discussion leader at the head. Two to three hours flew by without notice.

I was attracted to the studies and the discussions, the subjects fascinated me and still do.

The Beitler Street Synagogue was a Shull, Synagogue is too formal a name for a small house of prayer. When you entered it's courtyard, on the right side was the home of the Waldman family. Rabbi Waldman was the official 'Dayan' in a capacity like a Justice of the Peace for settling disputes, affairs among litigants. Rarely did Jews go to City Courts to adjudicate civil cases among themselves.

All the way back in this courtyard was the Shull; in this large room people congregated for the morning and evening prayers. The necessary Minyan quorum of ten men was never a problem. Before one entered the Shull, there was this ante room were you removed your coat and shook the rain off your shoes or boots. It was a place where people had a chance to greet one another before entering the Shull. In this space a few times a year, book vendors showed their collection of literary and prayer books on long tables. These were mostly old out-of-print books, which had been passed down from previous owners. In the community at large, congregants usually followed one of the two leading rabbinic scholars of the time; the Vizsnitzer or the Satmarer. The Rabbis had loyal Chassidim (followers). The Satmarer Rabbi's followers were ultra Orthodox, more so than the followers of Vizsnitzer Rabbi's, whose teaching was more modern and more contemporary. The difference between the Rabbis was such that their respective followers constantly fought verbal battles, claiming one being holier than the other.

Their fame traveled far and wide among the Chassidic communities. They were considered the wisest of that period. To spend a holiday at their respective Synagogue and listen to their favored Rabbi's teachings; that pilgrimage was equal to a lifetime achievement.

The Shull was open to all, membership was not required. Individuals would stop in for the obligatory Kaddish (a prayer for a departed family member), circumcisions (Brith Milah) and many other religious functions. This house of prayer was open around the clock.

I must have been 15-or-16 years old. It was not unusual for me to stop in for the evening (Mincha—Maariv) or (Shacharit—Musaf) morning prayers. Since my friends lived in the neighborhood the location was very convenient. Sunday was my free day, I had no school and used to take advantage of that free time. Before going on an excursion to the woods, playing soccer football, or rowing in the canal with Eddy Goldstein, I always went first to the morning prayer service.

On this particular Sunday morning the synagogue was crowded. Row after row all seats were taken; people standing in the aisles also crowded. The entire congregation was reciting Thilim (Psalms of David), with one voice we read all the Psalms, verse after verse without interjections.

I had participated in congregational prayers before but this was different. The chorus began the night before, men and boys were coming, others were leaving, but the recital continued. When I asked why, what was going on? I was told about this young man whose name I still remember, Hershi, who was mortally ill with high fever. Just as the Biblical King David prayed that God may grant him safety, peace and protection facing his enemies, so did the congregation petition the Almighty, to grant life to this young man. The Psalms are prayers of the afflicted, begging God's mercy and healing when overwhelmed by fear and helplessness. True, many died from all sorts of infectious diseases and for no known reasons others got better. This was years before antibiotic medicine was available.

In Hebrew school we were challenged to memorize all the 150 verses. At that early age I could recite many by heart in Hebrew and not fully understand the significance and beauty of that poetry.

On occasions when all known medicine had been exhausted without relief, the community stepped in and with unending prayer and devotion, tried to alter the fate of the individual and bring healing to the suffering. We always prayed, when nothing else worked we prayed more.

Our main synagogue was a beautiful building, built in the middle of the 18Th century. It definitely was a showcase for Jewish communal life. The interior was spacious with built-in mahogany benches all facing the Bima and the Arc. High above the Arc the sunlight filtered through large stained-glass windows. The second floor balcony was for women only. In the attic, the space below the roof was full of old torn books, prayer shawls, old study books and worn out tefilin with leather straps. Nothing was ever discarded into the trash bin. All items were considered sacred. The synagogue had a large yard. In the back there were a number of first to third grade class rooms each with different teachers. My dreaded teacher Herr Adler was no longer my teacher but was still teaching.

Rabbi Ullman's residence was across the road from the synagogue as was the Mikva (the communal ritual bathhouse) with steam room facility. My father, my brother and I the three of us went to the steam room often. It was hard for me to get used to go into a room full of hot steam and not be able to see the person who sat next to me. In town we had about five other smaller shulls, strategically located in Jewish neighborhoods.

My father was a member of a small congregation with a Rabbi from a nearby town called Magyaros; therefore he was called the Magyarosher Rabbi. This small shull was on the second floor of an old building. It consisted of two rooms, the smaller one for women, separated by a curtain from the larger room that was for men only. The main seating was on benches on both sides of two long tables and other seating arrangements.

On the Mizrach wall (eastern wall) between two windows the Ark housed two Torah scrolls. All the members contributed to a fund for the support of the Rabbi, his family, and for the maintenance of the synagogue. Those patrons who contributed more generously were seated closer to the Ark. The Rabbi had a wife and a thirty-year-old daughter. There was a time when several matchmakers were engaged to find a suitable spouse for her, finally they succeeded.

I remember the wedding; everyone was of the opinion that the match was made in heaven.

The Rabbi was very pleased to gain a son-in-law and a possible successor. The old Rabbi was very special to me, he was the most selfless person I ever knew. A man about sixty, perhaps older (at my age everybody over thirty was old then) with hardly any hair but a long flowing white beard and clear blue eyes. On a Friday evening the Rabbi led the congregation in prayer. The lectern was very close to the Ark. As was the custom, large candles brightly illuminated the Rabbi's sidur (prayer book). It was a very hot day and evening in July. To allow a breeze of fresh air, the two windows one on each side of the Ark, were kept open. A gust of wind blew the flames from the candles onto the Ark and the curtain caught on fire. We all stood in disbelief to see the Rabbi not move and continue the service as if nothing had happened. Fortunately someone who sat closer to the Ark extinguished the fire before it could do serious damage, but the Rabbi did not move or step aside before he finished the service.

On high holidays the congregation engaged a professional cantor who, with his two sons as choir boys, conducted the services. On most occasions when a portion of the Torah was read, the rabbi performed that reading. With one breath he would read an entire chapter. Often I stood nearby to observe and wonder how long the rabbi could hold his breath. On Rosh Hashanah before the Shofar (the rams horn) was blown, with a small entourage for company, the rabbi used to run about a kilometer to the Mikva and after the immersion, purified in mind and body, return quickly to the Shofar service.

He was not known so much for his scholarship as for extreme piety and for living an exemplary life.

One prayer above others is indelibly printed in my memory. On Yom—Kippur, when the congregation recites the Shema Kolenu prayer, my father standing with Talith draped over his head, reciting the prayer in a low voice almost to a whisper. "Hear our voice O Lord our God, be compassionate with us, hear our prayers, cast us not off in our old age, forsake us not, abandon us not, do not put us to shame. In Thee we trust, Lord our God." (translated from the Hebrew text)

Uncontrollable tears flowed down my father's face. *We believed in the existence of a living God with eyes and ears, we prayed to a God who listened to our prayers. On those occasions we believed and felt God's presence.*

My parents were truly religious. They taught us by example and always to be considerate of others, to help those in need and share with those less fortunate. My mother knew how to read and write in both Romanian and Hungarian. Along with keeping a kosher home and lighting candles on the eve of holidays, my mother's religion was based on kindness and doing good deeds in the practical sense. Middle class was an idea that did not exist then. My father worked hard to sustain his family. Living in Transylvania was not the land of opportunity. The constitutional monarchy of Romania was no worse than the other monarchies of Europe. State Welfare (safety net) did not exist. With an economy mostly agrarian the country could produce for the needs of its citizens. For high school and above education, was limited to those who could afford to pay. To live in the cities one needed to be in commerce, skilled in manual trades or in professions (doctors lawyers teachers or clergy) and there were the poor, more then a few in our town who needed help. Every Friday my mother prepared two wicker baskets, packed with fruits and vegetables, eggs, milk, chicken fat, a home baked chalah and other basic items. My mother knew a family that was in great need. As soon as I returned from school I was sent to deliver the baskets. The family lived in a small apartment on Magyar Street.

The father was an underemployed cantor without a permanent position. A few times a year and for the holidays he had a paying job at one of the small congregations. Except for an occasionally paid religious function there was no income. He relied on the kindness of others to support his wife and three children. The older was a very pretty girl, she was a little younger then I. At times I hoped I would see her but then I was really not comfortable bringing food for her family. If it were in reverse I would have been embarrassed, children should not be demeaned that way.

My summers were pleasant I learned to play chess. I was never very good at it but I enjoyed the game. My sport was football (soccer) and we always found an empty lot somewhere to play. In early summer we began with a good second hand ball. When inflated properly it had a good bounce and was easy to kick. By the end of the summer the ball had so many patches it could not hold air anymore. I also went on excursions with my friends on bicycle when my brother allowed me to use his, but mostly on foot. The country roads were lined with fruit trees. You could not go hungry all summer long.

The villagers were friendly, we often went in the direction of Jaad and the Borgos. In Bram Stoker's novel the main character, Jonathan Harker, in search of Count Dracula and his castle, begins his journey from Bistritz, my home town. After he spends a night at The Golden Crown a local hotel, he hires a driver with carriage and a team of horses to take him to the Borgo Pass and the Carpathian Mountains. The native superstitions expressed in the novel "Dracula" are timeless.

Our park had majestic old chestnut trees and endless promenades with benches and well tended flower beds everywhere. In center of the park was a large circular gazebo with a weathered shingled roof.

Every Saturday evening from May to September a military brass band would play popular melodies and finish the program with a military march.

The sports stadium was situated at the far end of the park. It served many functions throughout the year. 'Gloria' our soccer team had a good standing in the league. From early spring until the first frost a football match was played on most Saturday or Sunday afternoons.

During the school months the stadium was a public place for parades and gymnastic events, in particular on May 10, Romanian National Independence Day. Attendance was mandatory, we dressed in school uniforms, and we marched and waved the national flag of blue, yellow and red. In winter the goal posts were taken down, the field was flooded with water and allowed to freeze for ice skating. Skiing and skating were sports only for those who could afford the cost of the equipment, mainly the Saxons participated in this sport.

At the South end of the park, on the other side of the arched concrete footbridge, there was the German tennis club a private club. I had no idea what the rules of the game were, except the players wore white shorts and white tennis shoes, and hit a white ball over the net.

I went to high school every day except on Sundays and national holidays. The geography and Latin teachers were outspoken anti Semites. For written exams they usually chose a Saturday; since I didn't write on the Sabbath, I always got a failing mark. Grades were from 1 to 10, 5 was passing. To achieve a passing grade average, my oral exams had to be very good. I was an above average student and was committed to learning. Tuition for secondary school was expensive, I was not going to waste the hard earned money my father had to pay. My brother and sister also went to high school. I had a fair idea how much our parents sacrificed to give us an education.

Before an exam my friend Eddy Goldstein and I studied at his house. I often found him at the kitchen table with books and note pad in front of him; Eddy wasn't studying, he was reading a mystery novel from a book spread on his knees under the table. He had a complete collection of Sherlock Holmes detective stories translated into Romanian. Eddy was one of four children, an older sister and brother and a younger sister. On the Beitler Gasse, with an entrance from an alley to a courtyard.

The Goldstein family occupied the entire second floor. I remember these details because my grandmother lived in an apartment off that courtyard before she retired.

Eddy's father managed a lumber yard that bordered on the man-made canal that powered the turbines that generated the city's electric supply.

Every other year Eddy and his brother built a rowboat that we often paddled up and down the canal. The water level was regulated by a dam. We had to be very careful, when the dam was lowered or raised the water level would become dangerously rapid and the canoe was difficult to navigate. One time, before we could row back to home port, the water level dropped so fast that our canoe got stuck on the rocks. The poor fish had to find little patches of water between the rocks to survive.

Hedy Pasternak lived down the street from my father's shop; on her way home she had to pass in front of the store. She was blond with freckles, slender and wore thick eyeglasses. Most of the time I couldn't see the color of her eyes because she always closed them when she removed her glasses. She was fair, her skin was very light with freckles; in a way she was pretty. I often wanted to find an excuse to talk to her but didn't have the courage. There were times when I could not take my mind off her. Since we belonged to the same group of friends we saw each other often but I never told her how I felt about her. Then Simi Spitz who lived around the corner from City Hall. Very bright, very reserved, always thinking, hard to figure out, but friendly.

We greeted each other saying "servus" we addressed adults respectfully with "sarut mina"(in Romanian), "kezeit csokolom" (in Hungarian), "and kuss die hand "(in German), all meaning kiss your hand. In Yiddish there is no equivalent to match that greeting. Also, "Gruss Got" in German.

Then there was the mad professor's tea room on the Spital Gasse, next to the Fritch Movie Theater, an elegant tea room (there was no other like it) that served the best Viennese pastry on silver trays and tableware, imported teas served in fine china cups and saucers. When the street ladies discovered this fine shop regular customers stopped going in.

The young women began to steal, first the silver teaspoons, fine china cups and cake forks, and on top of that, when they began to walk out without paying which was very nominal to begin with, the professor had to close his tearoom.

He had been a retired professor. This enterprise may have been a noble idea, to have a place where his former colleagues and students could meet and discuss the daily events and finer points of life over a cup of a fine brand of tea and delicious pastry. That street front was his world, the store was long and narrow with a long counter with bar stools. For more intimate groups in the back, a few elegant round tables with glass tops and comfortable chairs. Above the area in back of the store was a second level; a wrought iron narrow winding staircase leading to his living space. He certainly planned and built for himself an ideal existence. When on the town he was known for being the most polite individual. As far as we knew he had no family. He greeted everyone with greatest respect and honor. I was in high school when my friends discovered that if you greeted the Professor saying "Guten-tag" (good day) his response was usually "Ich habe die ehre", (my honor) when greeted "Ich habe die ehre", his response was "Guten tag" and he always tipped his hat with a slight bow.

During summer vacation, to escape the heat of the city, on most Saturdays we roamed the wooded hills of the Schiefferberg located on the other side of the Bistrita River. We crossed the arched concrete foot bridge and in no time we enjoyed the cool forest. We used to follow a single path that brought us to the top, there in the middle of a large clearing was this big cabin constructed of local timber. Inside, the keeper sold refreshments by the bottle; sweet carbonated drinks and bottled beer from our local brewery. If my memory is correct it's there that I first drank the slightly bitter taste of beer, the opposite of carbonated sweet soda. On a hot day there was no more pleasant a place than the Schiefferberg. Adults of all ages also frequented, walking the trails between the forest trees.

The gentle professor also enjoyed the forest, leaning on his walking cane he occasionally stopped to listen to the birds. We followed the professor from afar, there were times when we found the professor motionless for many minutes, completely entranced by the surroundings.

We spent entire afternoons in the forest exploring new trails; only late afternoon hunger pains reminded us it was time to go down and leave for home. We were of one mind, next week if the weather permits we'll be back on the Schiefferberg. The professor was a genteel person, his head always covered with a black top hat. It didn't take long before his cloths appeared shabby, his walk had less of a stride, and his overall appearance became sad. He continued to live in that second floor space, but the front entrance with leaded stain glass doors was closed to the world outside. When in the street he no longer held his head high and stopped greeting people. After a while he was not seen at all, rumors had it that the Professor was in the poorhouse. We were all saddened to learn that this gentle, kind and generous person had become homeless.

My father's early training and practice in shoe design made him a fine artisan. With his flair for fashion, many well-dressed women in town wore his made-to-order shoes. His shoes were hand made; his employees were highly skilled. For his craft he used the finest and best tanned leathers available. He combined many exotic materials such as lizard, crocodile and a variety of snake skins. The small goat and calf skins leathers were custom tanned in fashion colors.

During the thirties the world economic depression had reached our part of Europe also. My father's upscale customers started to dwindle, and those he still had, could not pay their debts. Waiting two to four months and sometimes longer to get paid was not unusual. He could not rely anymore on the made-to-order women shoe business; he then decided to mass produce children's shoes. At the time boot makers who used very heavy and coarse leathers made shoes for children. By changing to softer and finer leathers the shoes would be welcomed in the marketplace.

To be competitive, instead of buying full skins at high prices per square foot, he bought high quality leather by the kilogram; leather pieces that were left over from large volume women's shoe manufacturers.

The first buy was two large burlap sacks of black leather pieces. My father created a few designs that allowed the patterns to interlock like a jigsaw puzzle. Employing this method of nesting, the cost of upper leather per unit was reduced by more than half.

It had been a long time since I saw my father so excited and hopeful. After school I offered my help in sorting out the leather pieces. He also found ways to reduce the cost of the other component parts as well. The children's shoes were lasted and finished by hand; the same way as the expensive women shoes was made.

For the task he employed additional skilled shoemakers. In the city there weren't enough customers for children shoes, my father had to take the product to other markets. Nasaud stands out in my memory, a town not too far from Bistrita. My father had the little shoes tied in pairs by their shoe laces, (shoes were not bagged or boxed) then packed in a large wooden crate made and used for that purpose only. Over two hundred pairs were packed in that wooden crate. On one occasion I went along to help out.

On top of a horse drawn cart we traveled all night. I think that was the last time I traveled that way. We left before sunset and arrived at dawn, just in time to set up our stand. It had to be on a Wednesday or a Thursday, definitely not on a Tuesday because Tuesday was the big market day in my home town and my father would not have been away on that day. I observed how people arrived; they came from every corner of the square; they walked on foot in groups of two or more, women with children, many young women dressed in their best national dress. Farmers brought their produce to the market; oxcarts loaded high with sacks of corn, wheat, others with live stock, piglets, geese, ducks, eggs. Other merchants set up large stands with clothes, hats, yard goods, colorful ribbons, fabrics and linens; other stands with work shoes for men and women and high-laced dress shoes for women.

There were stands with cooked foods, roasted pork, sausages, breads, delicious sweet pastries, fruits and vegetables in season.

I remember the tall man in colorful national dress, a pure white linen long shirt outside his trousers, embroidered in colorful patterns, who had a stand, an average size table covered with hand made wooden spoons of every shape and size, some with motifs in bright red, yellow and blue the colors in the Romanian flag, hand painted on them. They were artfully carved and not expensive at all. No one bargained as was the custom in buying and selling other products.

At our stand to try on shoes, mothers held their children in their arms. For some children it was their first pair. The little shoes were priced at about 1/3 less than the market charged. My father's customers were pleased with glove soft leather shoes for their children. It was an amazing day, we practically sold out our entire inventory.

At the same time back home my father did not neglect the custom-made women shoe business but became more selective and served customers who could pay their bills. After school I would go to the shop to watch my father design and cut shoe patterns. I liked to draw, mostly with pencil or charcoal stick. Other than water color, many of today's products used for drawing in color had not been developed yet. I didn't know then, that in the future I would fall back and expand on what I had learned from my father.

Family portraits, all were in my aunt's possession in Brooklyn, NY; She gave them to me since I had none.

Photos of streets and buildings in Bistrita are from after the war,

My Aunt & My Mother

My Mother

Parents Wedding Portrait

Family Porttrait 1925—I was expected

Grandparents wth Bumi & Irena

My sister, me & brother (Left to Right)

Irena in HS uniform

Me—Age 12

Bumi & My Father

Irena & me at house

High School Friends

Irena—16 years old

Bumi—20 years old

My father 1941

Mother & Father at house

Our House

Bistrita

Chapter 2

YEARS OF AGONY

In 1940 the Iron Guard, the Fascist Party of Romania, forced King Carol to abdicate. That act in itself did not satisfy the Axis from breaking Romania apart. On August 30Th 1940, the Vienna Accord between Germany and Italy ceded northern Transylvania to Hungary. The change was unexpected, most people were bewildered; how can people adjust to such change? Without a fired shot an entire territory was divided in two. The Hungarian minority was delighted to become part of Hungary, on the other side the Romanians were devastated. Within a few days the transition took place. I remember, at the age of 14, I was standing on the sidewalk in front of my father's shop watching fierce looking Hungarian Hussars on horseback with plumed hats and drawn swords ride towards the military camp that was vacated by the Romanians the day before.

The change affected me greatly. My high school was no longer Romanian. The school administration was replaced with Hungarian teachers, the official language was now Hungarian. The event was traumatic to all. Our parents the World War I generation spoke Hungarian but the rest, Jews and Romanians alike we had limited language skills in Hungarian. From the court house, city hall, the police department, all the officials were replaced. All the streets were renamed in Hungarian. My mother and father, since they were of the First World War generation they already spoke Hungarian with each other. In our presence they spoke Yiddish, outside our home we spoke Romanian, some Hungarian, German, whatever language the occasion required. It was a very confusing time, my ability to speak, read and write Hungarian was very limited. To continue my education I had to take private lessons. I was unhappy about it but had no choice.

My father was pleased with the change of government. His early life before the First World War had been under Hungary. Now my father and my sister Rifku were excited about their planned trip to Budapest.

Compared to a few years earlier, oddly my father's business had much improved. He prepared the shop so it could function without him for a while and off they went. They had a wonderful time in Budapest. We received many picture post cards from them. On their return my sister told us about all the exciting places they had visited. They went to the museum, to the opera, to the Dohany Templom, which was the largest Synagogue in Budapest, and the world famous lanchid (chain bridge) over the Danube River. For my father it was going back to the place where he was once young and happy; but Budapest was no longer the city he once knew so well and loved. The entire country gradually came under Hungarian Fascists and German Nazi influence. I must plead ignorance, for during those few years from 1940 to 1944, the change of Government the gradual changes in culture in our lives, the gradual changes were incremental, slightly noticed. My father must have been aware as when he returned from Budapest he described how Budapest had changed as any other city might change after 20 some years. We lived under Romanian anti Semitism, then under Hungarian rule we did not expect much better. During those four years we must have known of the daily events in other parts of Europe. Did we believe that those bad things wont happen to us? Did we suffer a kind of collective Amnesia for lack of a better word or a collective helplessness that infected every community where Jews lived?

That summer I visited my ten cousins, they were the children of my father's older sister. They lived in Zalau, a half-day's distance by bus. My uncle Markovich was a baker; they lived in a rented big sprawling house with the bakery toward the street. The house was situated almost at the top of the hill. Steps were part of the sidewalk, a flat walk, then steps, then a flat walk again, alternating up and up to the top of the street. That in itself was not too bad but their drinking water came from a communal fountain at the bottom of the hill. During the day my cousins and I took turns carrying jugs of water uphill. It was hard to imagine my cousins carrying water every day.

My uncle Markovich was a good baker, his freshly baked bread sold out daily. Although they were poor they appeared to be a happy family. One day I went to the movies with three of my cousins. Hungarian teenagers who sat in back of us, were hurling anti Semitic verbal insults at us. Back home I had not experienced that kind of behavior yet. There was nothing we could do about it. In spite of all that I had a great time with my cousins. I stayed for a week, on my return home my cousin Ibi came back with me. She was my age. At first it was to be just for a short visit, but she continued to live with us as a member of the family.

Under Hitler, Germany unleashed a Blitz-Krieg, a lightning war of aggression against her neighbors. England and France were poorly prepared to defend themselves, let alone to come to the aid of the smaller and weaker countries. Poland, Denmark, Belgium, Holland, Czechoslovakia, the Balkan states; except for Austria. The Austrians welcomed Hitler with open arms; all the others made feeble attempts to defend themselves. With the Non Aggression pact of 1939 between Germany and the Soviet Union, came the division of Poland. Later on, Hungary and Romania, ruled by fascists, became de facto allies of Nazi Germany. Within a few years, the exception of Sweden and Switzerland, two neutral countries, from the Baltic to the Mediterranean, all of Europe came under Nazi German influence and domination. As for details and explanations I leave that to historians who are better equipped to analyze and explain the whys and causes for the events of that period.

To hear news from the West, we listened to BBC broadcasts in Romanian and Hungarian. It was good to hear news other than German propaganda but BBC radio informed us poorly about the fate of the Jews in countries occupied by Nazi Germany. By word of mouth we heard terrible things, the news was too terrifying we chose not to believe any of it. We lived in constant fear and we prayed and hoped that we'd be saved somehow. We still hoped and believed in miracles.

At the main intersection in the center of town, we had a newly built kiosk with a newsstand, on the same location where the old building used to be. This was a modern concrete structure. Newspapers and magazines were displayed in a circular fashion all around the kiosk; without obstruction one could find the paper or magazine of choice. We had no local press. Our printed news came from Cluj (Koloswar) the capitol of Transylvania; it arrived every afternoon at five. Outside the kiosk we used to wait for the daily newspapers to arrive. To be informed objectively was impossible. The press was censored and of little use. The new kiosk had another practical feature: under the newsstand a circular staircase led down to a public W.C. with wash basins and flush toilets. It was the only outdoor public toilet in town.

After the June 1941 surprise German invasion of Soviet Russia, our lives began to change for the worst. In the past we were exposed to a measure of anti-Semitism. We were used to being humiliated, rudely spoken to, falsely accused and called uncomplimentary names. There were always isolated cases of outright hostility toward us; yet collectively we were never in serious life threatening danger. We all knew about the pogroms in Russia, and the anti-Semitic venom spewed from the church pulpits on Easter Sundays. Ignorance reigned in many places. It was easy to hate the Jew who was not known as a neighbor, a fellow worker, or a fellow student. That is when the phrase became so popular there also "My best friends are Jews"

In our community we participated in every constructive way. We were good citizens and contributed to the general good. Rarely did a Jew commit a crime or even remotely be involved in one. To the best of my recollection there were no Jews in our town's jail. In spite of all that, Jews were always under a microscope. We were 'Christ Killers', a 2000-year-old stigma, and an accusation that we were not guilty of. (In recent years on his visit to Jerusalem, Pope John II, has personally asked for forgiveness for the mistreatment of the Jewish people in the last 2000 years)

One day, an endless column of Russian prisoners of war was marched through our town. They were in terrible condition with serious injuries, head wounds, limping, supporting each other, in torn uniforms, many barefoot, others with rags wrapped around their feet. The reality of war was right before our eyes. We looked on in disbelief. Is this what the mighty Soviet soldier had become? Seeing these helpless men frightened me I am sure the site equally shocked others. From a distance some townspeople threw loves of bread, baked potatoes, all kinds of food items to them; however the German guards did not allow the towns people to get near the prisoners. It was obvious that they were

47

treated badly. Guarded by Wehrmacht soldiers they were marched to the sports stadium and held for days in that open space without shelter.

America had not been in the war yet, only the Soviet Union was fighting the Nazis in Europe. On the Russian front the Germans advanced nothing could stop them. It was depressing to look at the map of Europe and see how far the Germans had advanced; with not much resistance they reached Stalingrad. No one was aware how or when the Soviet prisoners were taken away; one day they were just gone.

For several years beginning in 1941 many Saxon young men from our area, began to go to Germany as volunteers to the Wehrmacht or the SS branch of the military. It was no surprise to see so many Saxons volunteer. Since they spoke a German dialect they always considered themselves Germans. Prussians, German ambitions were always in their political background. German propaganda, Hitler's fiery speeches, and his military successes all over the continent and the ever-growing Nazi youth movements were very difficult to resist. Now they saw their own destiny tied to Nazi Germany.

Not everyone was accepted into the SS. Only the most privileged could join that special branch. My friend and neighbor Ziggy who lived in the house next to ours also volunteered. As children we played in each other's home almost every day. His father Arthur Hoch owned a dry goods store located under the arches of the Sugalete in center of town.

Ziggy had no mother at home, she left about five years earlier; she went on a trip to Buenos Aires (Argentina) and never returned. Occasionally she sent picture post cards to Ziggy. Once or twice I asked if he had heard from his mother but he rarely talked about her. It was a sensitive subject to talk about. I was not surprised, he missed his mother. His father was a very strange person, at home he always walked around without any clothes on. I did not like to visit Ziggy when his father was home. Otherwise he was a good neighbor. After work he seldom left the house he rarely had visitors. The Hoch's house also extended like ours, with entrances on both streets. The Elizabeta side of the house its windows were always shuttered and closed.

The Hochs occupied the whole house except for one room with two windows on Elizabeta Street. The woman who lived there was a clerk at the Fritch movie house's ticket office. One thing we knew about this woman that she was huge, her head was big and every part of her was abnormally large. She was known as the elephant lady. She smoked a lot. There were always cigarette ashes below her window where she probably emptied her ashtray.

A few months later I met Ziggy on our street. He wore a German army uniform. I rushed toward him and greeted him warmly, Servus Ziggy 'you look great in your uniform" I said, I saw a friend and neighbor not a German soldier. His response in German was crude and hostile. He said to me "Du bist ein dreckige Jude" (You're a dirty Jew) I'm not supposed to talk to you. I was shocked by his remarks and he caught me by surprise. I didn't know how to answer, I just walked away. How could he have changed so much? From where did all that hatred come from?

When I described the incident to my father he was very saddened. He told me that similar encounters had happened to him also. Senior Hoch had a brother with wife and children who lived four houses up the street. The older son was my age, also Ziggy's age. They went to private schools. We were on friendly terms, his mother was a Hungarian woman.

The two Hoch brothers were in the same kind of business, evidently competing with each other, and they did not talk to each other, and the cousins also didn't speak to each other. I also remember that Ziggy's cousin did not volunteer to help the Reich.

Our friendly neighbors became indifferent, Hungarian fascists and Nazi youth gangs, dressed in brown shirts, (that was the uniform for young Nazis) began to attack elderly Jews, women and children. It became dangerous to walk in the street. Every day someone else got beaten up. On main streets or on side streets, any time of day it was risky to be out. We were increasingly forced to stay at home. Since 1938, newsreels in movie houses showed Nazi parades in Berlin, large gatherings of people listening to the barking speeches by Hitler. Spectacles never seen before, it seemed as if entire armies of uniformed Nazi soldiers with Nazi banners were marching to Nazi Army bands. No wonder the local Neo Nazis and the Fascist population were swept up, believing in the idea that they also belonged to the superior Aryan race.

First came the annexation of the Sudeten provinces of Czechoslovakia, then in 1938 the Vienna Anschlus (Annexation) with the Austrians literally begging to be included into Nazi Germany. Not to mention the humiliating conference with Chamberlain, the prime minister of England in Munich, with Chamberlain's meaningless phrase "Peace In Our Time" on his return to London; Diplomacy with Hitler was worthless. Nazi expansionist aggression to the west of Europe included France, Belgium, Holland, Denmark, and to the East, Germany divided Poland with the Soviet Union. We witnessed all of this unfolding in front of our eyes, in the press, radio and newsreels. That nightmare had overtaken us and was all around us. Nazi youth organizations held rallies, Saxons from villages around the city came to town. With swastika arm bands and Nazi flags, they marched and sang Nazi songs. On a few occasions we got into fist fights with them and to our satisfaction we bloodied a few of their noses also. The Nazi youth gangs were overwhelming, the local police were impotent or unwilling to control them, and they ignored their comings and goings.

To this foreign Nazi influence, the local Fascist movement also became more vocal than before.

We had two movie houses in town. Barahoglu operated the larger cinema, a man of Turkish origin; this man and my father were on friendly terms. The movie house had a balcony and a loge section also. There was a separate walkway to the loge. To exit after the performance, we could reach the street through an alley. The film was "Jud Suss" a very anti Semitic German production based on a novel by Leon Feuchtwanger, or Fruchtwanger. When Mr. Barahoglu, owner manager of the cinema saw me with my friends at the box office window, he came over and led us to a loge box. I was impressed by his generosity, our tickets were for general seating. Evidently he didn't want us Jewish boys to be exposed to possible heckling or worse. I had no idea what the film was about. The Nazi portrayal of the character was revolting, a propaganda film made to stir hatred towards Jews. Obviously Mr. Barahoglu had no choice in showing or not showing the film.

Day after day, anti Semitic propaganda was fierce. To hear world news, we listened to BBC London radio news programs. We were forbidden to listen to short wave radio, my brother and I took turns, while one listened the other stood watch outside our house. The news we heard was not good and we became more fearful every day.

The Soviet armies were falling back, abandoning their cities and towns. The Hungarian national press and radio had accounts of glorious German successes on all fronts. My father opened his shop every day, his shop had not been closed yet. When he went to buy supplies from businesses he had patronized for many years, as if he were invisible, no one paid attention to him. Then he began to close his shop earlier, he had one employee left. He feared for his safety. We did not leave our home after dark. We became increasingly fearful and depressed. The miracles we hoped for were late in coming. The war was not going to end soon.

The Hungarian government, under Horthy in Budapest, was pressured by the Fascists in Parliament to act against the Jewish population. It didn't happen all at once; little by little, day by day, one restriction followed by another, reduced our ability to live normal lives.

And then the Nazis came . . . On March 19, 1944 the German military occupied Hungary.

The "Nuremberg Laws" began to be enforced with a vengeance. Every day new and more restrictive laws were posted on the walls all over town. We were not allowed in public places, some businesses were confiscated, we were not allowed to leave town, along with the humiliation of being singled out as a people without rights, association with non Jews was reduced considerably. Most encounters became strongly anti-Semitic, full of hatred and ill will. There were accounts of men taken off trains and busses by Fascists militias. (Hungarians were Fascists Germans were Nazis) Those who were suspect were forced to drop their pants. Circumcised man were arrested and delivered to the SS or the Gestapo. German military units were passing through the city every day. One such Wehrmacht military unit had parked its vehicles on our street and was there a whole day. A few of them came through our gate and into the house. The soldiers were polite, they asked for water; my mother guided them to the outdoor fountain, a cast iron fountain with a handle to pump up water from the well. In other places they confiscated whatever they wanted. Apparently they were on their way to the Russian front.

The German military stored hundreds of steel drums with fuel on a field a few kilometers outside the city. To camouflage them, they were covered with evergreen branches. The Jewish community leaders who dealt with the authorities had to provide groups of young men to work for the German military. For about a week I also worked at one of those forced outings. German military trucks took us to a pine forest, there we cut down branches to cover the field of oil drums. A German soldier who had recently been transferred from Lithuania, informed us about what had happened to the Lithuanian

Jews. He was surprised to see us still relatively free. He told us that the Lithuanian Jews had long been liquidated.

I did not understand the meaning of the word "liquidated" I never heard that word applied that way before.

I remember the feeling I had. I did not believe him, none of us did. The stories he told us were too gruesome, we thought he just wanted to frighten us. When I returned home that evening I told my father what I had heard.

A few days later an ordinance ordered all Jews to turn in their radios, it was considered an instrument of espionage, they had to be delivered to the police station. Since last December my brother was not home anymore, being of military age he had been drafted to work in a labor brigade for the Hungarian Army. Instead of regular military service, Jews were given picks and shovels and assigned to road work, digging trenches on the Russian front and all kinds of other manual labor to support the Hungarian military. By then Hungary was subordinate to German rule.

I remember how I cried all the way to the police station. I loved that radio. My father bought it because it had a short wave band, it was a "Telefunken" brand radio, made in Germany. The radio was the only link to the outside world, without a radio we were completely cut off. A few days later all Jewish professionals were arrested; doctors, teachers, all were accused of being spies and/or Communists. They were not spies, and certainly they were not Communists. When the women inquired about their spouses they were told they're being interrogated . . . Each was told a different story. We never saw the men again. Their properties were confiscated, their families suffered untold hardships. The Fascists knew that by removing the intelligentsia, the potential leaders first, they could deal with the rest of us more effectively.

The owner of the building where my father's store was, had been to America in the 1920 s. During prohibition, he made a fortune bootlegging whiskey, then returned to Romania, and invested in real-estate. He bought rental properties in Bistrita and lived on a farm with hundreds of acres of land. At home his wife would not let him drink alcohol.

He loved his whiskey; to have a few drinks he used to drive into town in his own carriage with two magnificent horses. Before he rode home he always visited my father. On his last visit he was very drunk. He pleaded with my father to listen to him, the things he'd been hearing were bad, and he offered to help us, hide all of us on his farm. Had he not been so drunk perhaps my father would have accepted his offer.

And so we existed for a few more weeks. We just didn't know what to do, there was nowhere to go and no one to turn to for help. Forbidden to leave town, we were ordered to wear yellow arm bands. I was expelled from school and my father had to close his shop. With all the restrictions in place we still hoped that we could survive somehow. My father's cash savings would last us for a while. Considering the way the war was going, by then the German armies had been defeated at Stalingrad, driven out of most of Russia, the defeat of Germany was a near certainty and with some luck we hoped the war would be over soon.

Then, rumors of imminent disaster came from all sources. As a precaution my father wanted me to help him hide some of our valuables. 60,000 Pengo Hungarian money, a considerable sum my father had saved, and 3,200 American Dollars my father kept in a metal box under the floor boards under the closet, in the corner of my parents' bedroom. Next to our kitchen, in back of our large storeroom, there was another smaller pantry room. Inside that windowless room with a compacted dirt floor, we stored a barrel of home made wine, a sack of flour, a sack of walnuts, onions, on a shelf jars of plum preserves that my mother had prepared the previous fall and other items we put there in haste. To assure the room's secrecy my father and I moved a heavy large pantry closet from the kitchen. We placed it so that it completely covered the entrance to that smaller pantry room. We knew it was not a good hiding place, but for the moment it was all we could do. My mother had a long gold necklace and two gold rings and my sister had a few gold pins.

My father did not want to upset them, they were frightened enough without having to suggest the necessity of hiding their jewelry. My father's gold chain and pocket watch; his beautifully engraved detachable prayer shawl, made of sterling silver and a few other pieces of jewelry we placed in an earthen pot. We dug a hole in the yard near the woodshed and buried it. Only the two of us knew its hiding place. It's very hard for me to recollect and reconstruct those last hours of freedom. I tried to prepare myself mentally, but what was to come was unthinkable.

Chapter 3

SEPARATION

On May 3, 1944 before dawn, heavy knocks on our kitchen door woke us. An armed group of Hungarian Fascists in civilian clothes was outside. We were ordered to dress; they allowed us to take a few things we could pack in a hurry and not much else. In our confusion we took very little. In front of our house on the Regina Maria Street, an open military truck with another Jewish family already on it was waiting for us. I will ask the reader to stop for a moment and think of how vulnerable and defenseless we were then. Humiliated and powerless, my parents, my old grandmother (my mother's mother), my cousin Ibi, my sister Rifku and I we left our home and climbed onto the truck. All though we had been prepared for days for something to happen but when the moment came, when we heard the order at our door to pack up and leave; without locking the door behind us we left our home our possessions our life, as if we had never existed.

Vasile, a former apprentice in my father's shop, whom I had not seen for some time, was standing on the sidewalk next to the truck. He appeared out of nowhere, we looked at each other without saying a word, there wasn't time. As the truck pulled away, I wanted to give him something to remember me by. I had this one inch square gold framed wrist watch with a leather strap, I took it off my wrist and tossed it to him, he caught it and called out "I'll take care of it for you"

Very quickly the truck was driven to two other Jewish homes on our street. One of the families was the Nussbachers. They must have had a list with names and addresses.

When the truck was full, we were taken to an open field, a slowly rising hill outside the city. The area was familiar to me, I had once skied on that hill with a borrowed pair of skies.

The field was surrounded by a high wire fence and guarded by young Hungarian Fascists, all civilians armed with rifles. I suspected they were all volunteers. Truckloads, one after another, brought entire families from the city and from neighboring villages. By the end of the day the so-called Ghetto was full.

The Ghetto. Right from the start, even on the most temporary basis, our needs were great. Shelter, food, water, sanitary needs all were few or non existent. Boys and girls of my age we organized work brigades. We worked long hours to help alleviate the severe conditions. Confiscated lumber from my friend Goldstein Eddie's father's lumber yard was used to erect makeshift shelters. We hastily organized communal kitchens, food items from Jewish owned stores and homes were brought in to feed the people. We stood in line for water, for bread, for soup, there were long lines to the outhouses, and we stood in line for everything.

I worked with the latrine brigade. In designated areas we dug trenches, just to make existence bearable we all worked to the point of exhaustion. At night the screams of young children, cries of babies, filled the air throughout the ghetto. Our make shift housing had no walls, two or more families together was normal. At night, exhausted from working all day, I wrapped myself in a blanket and looked for a place to lie down on the ground. Usually I fell asleep but not for long. I awoke gripped by fear and terror I could not shake. I could hardly wait for day break. I choose not to describe in more detail the daily events in that forsaken place, because there are no words that can express the horror I felt, an entire people to be abandoned on that hillside like worthless trash.

Nobody knew how long we would have to stay there. It was useless to ask anybody, nobody knew anything. We all felt like caged animals. We wondered how we could have come to this. People we associated with, most as friends and neighbors, how could they turn against us without cause? We could not understand how Nazi propaganda could turn into such hatred. After long hours of work, when with my parents I hardly spoke with them.

Seeing the fear in their eyes, I was determined not to add to their anxieties. The community could not possibly live under those conditions for long. I feared people were going to die.

Day after day our routine was the same; stand in line for soup, another line for bread, endless lines for everything. The trenches we dug for latrines soon had to be covered with dirt and new ones dug. The days were warm in the sun, but the nights were damp and cold. On clear nights I could see the lights of our town. I did not dare think that I might never see my home again. One day, a few of us were assigned to go to the city and bring back a truckload of bread. While we were loading the truck at the bakery, thoughts of escape crossed my mind. I had an automatic four color pencil. I offered my pencil to one of the guards. I explained my intentions to him and for some unexplained reason and to my surprise he agreed. I gave him my automatic pencil, within a minute or two the truck was out of my sight and I found myself walking around the corner of the street away from the bakery. It felt so good, in my mind I began to imagine what to do next. Now I was free but had no place to go; I hardly considered the consequences. This sense of freedom didn't last long; my thoughts turned to my parents. What will they think, how will they handle difficult situations by themselves? They'll suffer because of my absence. My decision to escape was not thought out well. I decided to return to the bakery, before anyone even noticed that I was gone I helped loading the truck, and returned to the Ghetto. I never told my parents about my attempted escape, I was glad to be back with them.

Days passed without much conversation between us. Disbelief to the degree of helplessness, abandoned and overwhelmed with panic my mother began to express her fears. All she wanted to know was why? She kept asking why are they doing this to us? (as if there was a logical explanation) What crimes have we committed to deserve such treatment? How does God allow such horrible things happen to so many innocent people? She cried bitterly unable to stop herself.

My sister Rifku in despair also crying, pleaded with me to assure our mother that what was going on was only temporary and soon we'll all be going home. I tried to assure her but she felt it was going to get worse. She prayed that our suffering would end soon. In spite of all the humiliation, she still believed as we all did, in common human decency, that people just don't do such heartless things to others.

My father was very disappointed also. He had been a loyal citizen; during First World War, while serving in the Austro-Hungarian army, he endured all sorts of hardships. He understood that in time of war certain people are less equal than others and some rights could be denied. There could be arrests, severe penalties against those individuals whom the state does not trust; but wholesale arrests of families with children young and old, without being accused of anything, that kind of tyranny was unprecedented. When basic human rights were denied us, no one could foresee the result to such brutality.

My grandmother believed that by self denial and personal sacrifice one could change one's fate. She had always fasted every Monday and Thursday, now she refused to eat even the little food that was rationed. Most of the day and night she crouched in a corner on a small makeshift pillow on the cold bare ground. At night she shivered.

I returned from my attempted escape to be with my family to help them, to be with them, but what encouragement could I offer? I was so frustrated. Work to exhaustion was the only thing I could do, just not to have to think about our situation. My cousin Ibi also worked at different posts. We all did our share. The weather continued to be kind to us. In the open with so very little protection, rain would have been disastrous.

After about two long weeks, we were loaded onto trucks. Some survivors claim that the ghetto was liquidated in two transports, others said that there were three transports. I have no knowledge of how many truck transports they used, to take us to the rail station.

The streets were mostly deserted. I wanted so much to believe that the towns people were hiding from our view, because they also felt helpless, or maybe because of their sense of shame or guilt. Some of the Romanians and Hungarians may have been sympathetic to our plight, but not the Saxons (Folk Deutche) they supported the Nazi causes; their sons and daughters volunteered to serve the SS as my former neighbor and friend Ziggy did. As the trucks passed on the street in front of our home, I had a horrible feeling, I kept looking back until it was out of sight. When we reached the end of the Regina Maria Street the column of trucks turned right, toward the railroad station.

Along the tracks about 1/4 mile away from the station the trucks came to a stop, then soon after we were ordered to get off. Without a complaint not even a groan, we obeyed every order; we did what we were told. We unloaded the trucks we helped each other take down the few belongings we still had. The empty trucks left, and we stood there waiting. It's impossible to imagine how we felt what our thoughts were. We were very quiet, in shock and bewildered. I remember the despair, I could feel it all around me, and my father's expression was overcome with panic. Shortly after, a cattle car train slowly inched its way toward us, the cars creaked and clanged, then abruptly stopped in front of us.

A new reality set in. All we hoped for was, that our family would not be separated. I don't remember exactly how many cars were coupled together; there were many. The doors slid open and we were told to climb onto them. Up to that moment we hoped we would be relocated somewhere to work in some capacity, and for that reason families were not separated. Once we were loaded into the cattle cars, each tightly crammed beyond capacity, the Nazis betrayed their intent.

Soon as we were loaded, the doors were slid shut and latched from the outside. We began to sense Nazi brutality, we saw the face of evil.

Everybody tried to bring along some belonging, no matter how insignificant, people held on to a bundle or a small piece of luggage. With so little space, personal belongings began to create problems. I tried to count heads, I wanted to know how many we were in that cramped space. Some of the older people like my grandmother, were sitting in their places yet every time I counted I came up with a different number. There were about 65 to 70 people in our car, including two young mothers, one with one baby the other with two. There were without their husbands, the men were of military age like my brother, also serving in labor brigades for the Hungarian Army. There were two slop buckets at opposite corners of the car. The cattle car had a small open space for a window; it was cross-bared with iron rods. Those who were close to that small opening stretching on their toes, could look out. At times the train slowed down to a stop, but always not in or near a train station.

We didn't know how far we had traveled, or where we were going. For the first few hours, as if we had all lost our voices, there was an eerie calm and complete silence. I could see the tracks between the spaces of the floor boards. The rhythmic sound of the wheels, had a hypnotic, lulling effect on me, and perhaps on others also.

This calm did not last long, children started to cry and the parents were unable to comfort them. There was so little space, some of the older adults began to moan from their pain and discomfort. The crying, moaning and complaining became so loud, people lost control. Some had more baggage than others, all of which took space and it became a source of conflict. Some had thoughts of where we were headed; all sorts of ideas were brought forth. We voiced more questions than we could find answers to. We considered all possibilities, after a while we realized the futility, the uselessness of arguing about where we were being taken.

As the day turned into evening it began to get dark. The first night was very long, those who were crowded in the middle of the wagon were warm, by contrast, and those along the walls of the wagon were cold. The wind blew through the spaces in the walls and floor-boards.

There was no water to drink, the buckets became full of excrement and urine; simple modesty disappeared. Men and women dropped their pants to do what they had to do. The mood changed by the minute. One moment you could hear outbursts of despair, then anger, some prayed, others cursed. They blamed our community leaders who negotiated with the Hungarian authority for not telling us the truth. Finally we realized it was just the beginning of our destruction.

What evil devices have they created? Without the slightest resistance, they arrested an entire people. Obediently we left our homes, our possessions, and our existence; passively we allowed them to do this to us. Around me I saw my family, my friends and neighbors too frightened even to cry. Nobody complained anymore. We had adjusted to the discomforts, the pains, the stench, nothing mattered anymore.

Next day for the most part we were all quiet, the adults accepted the situation as it was, but the children were hungry and thirsty. We realized we could do absolutely nothing to change our condition. No longer were we curious to know where we were, or where the train was going, all we wanted was, to arrive anywhere and be able to leave, to get out from that place we were locked up in.

AUSCHWITZ

About 2 a.m. of the second night, the train came to a sudden stop. I heard dogs barking outside. Somehow I had the feeling we had arrived at our destination; from the outside our wagon door was unlatched and pushed wide open. Loud voices in German soon became commands; many SS officers hurriedly walked along the side of the train with whips in their hands, shouting commands at us. "Heraus, heraus ferfluchte Juden, heraus!" (Out, out cursed Jews out!) The blinding bright flood lights aimed at the wagons made everybody even more horrified. The orders were to get off immediately and leave everything behind.

In disbelief we looked at each other, scared out of our minds, what else can we do but obey. In the back of the wagon (cattle car) some just began to stir, still hesitating. My mother and sister, I never saw them so frightened before. As if the air from our lungs had been sucked out; we were speechless. We did not expect a welcoming party on arrival but, this was more frightening than my worst nightmare. To this moment I can't remember how my grandmother got off the wagon.

As we jumped off the wagons, SS men swung their whips indiscriminately. Within minutes all had jumped off the train with only the clothes we had on. We hardly left the wagons when men in striped uniforms speaking Polish and Yiddish jumped onto the wagons and unloaded everything we left behind.

They performed with such efficiency that it was obvious they had done that task before. Women and children were ordered to cross to the other side of the tracks; within a few minutes we were separated from them.

We were ordered to line up and walk towards the head of the train. Across the tracks the women were also walking in the same direction. My father and I we found ourselves holding hands and walking slowly. I looked across to the other side and saw my mother holding a baby in her arms, evidently she was helping the woman who had the two babies. I looked for my sister Rifku, cousin Ibi, and grandmother but I did not see them. Even though bright flood lights were projected on us, on all of us; when I glanced again toward my mother, I could not find her either. I had my overcoat on, my father wore his hat and coat. In my coat pocket I had a small jar of strawberry jam a fine Hungarian brand from (Kecskemet) the one item I still had from home. As we walked, I spooned that jam with my fingers into my mouth. Out of fright I ate most of it; that sweet fruity substance caused me to faint later.

It was not difficult to figure out the process. I could see ahead of the line a point where a selection was taking place. The very old, the very young and the sick were sent to the right and fast vanishing from sight. The rest were moving forward to the left.

As we approached the spot where the selection took place, I stepped forward, without hesitation the selector ordered me to the left. I took a few steps and waited for my father. I heard the selector ask my father "konnen sie arbeiten?" (can you work?) Had he answered hesitatingly he would have been sent to the gas chambers. My father's reply was a loud "jawohl" (yes), (that reply was a typical reply to an officer in WW I) there was a delay of a few seconds, and the selector then looked in my direction and saw my arm stretched out towards my father as if I was waiting for him. He then ordered my father in my direction.

We passed another hurdle . . . and were still together. The air was warm, the flood lights made it impossible to see the sky. In a short distance flames spewed out of chimneys, the odor was strong, the air smelled of burning flesh. I still had no idea about the existence of crematoria and their functions.

We caught up with those ahead of us who then stood before a huge pile of clothes. We were ordered to strip completely and toss our clothes onto the pile, but we were allowed to keep our shoes. I undressed quickly and stood there naked, my father took longer, and his suspenders got in his way. An inmate in striped clothes who stood in back of us, beat my father with a black stick over the head and back. That was the first time of many that my father was hit. Later we learned that those with the hard black rubber clubs were inmates with special duties and often with privileges. They were Kapos selected by the Nazis for their ability to beat and do cruel things to their fellow inmates. My father fell to the ground and to avoid getting beaten again, I ripped the clothes off him as fast as I could. I helped him up and again we had to run to catch up with those ahead. My father had a hernia, in haste he let go of his truss, it was a big mistake; it's possible he could have kept it but now it was too late. His right hand was now constantly at his side supporting that weak spot.

Now, all naked except for our shoes, we entered a dimly lit passageway. On either side barbers also inmates, crudely shaved our heads and genital areas. Before I reached the barbers I fainted and fell at my father's feet. When I came to, my father was kneeling over me, he helped me up and together we walked over to the barbers. I had never fainted before or since. After we were shaven and showered we were given pants and jacket outfits, the striped outfit of all the inmates.

Exhausted from the long train trip, and the night of horrors we had just lived through; from persons with names and identities, in a few hours we were transformed into people whose existence depended entirely on the will of the Nazis around us. Life or death was in their hands. No wonder the notorious Dr. Mengele was called the angel of death. With a motion of his finger, he selected people for the gas chambers, or to be sent to labor camps. For all I know he could have been the selector that night.

The women also went through a selection process. Later we learned that those who were not selected for work, men, women and children, immediately after selection, were sent to the gas chambers. If one could imagine a fiery hell on earth, that was Auschwitz.

I could go on and try to describe the first impressions of this demonic place, but no words are fit in any language. It is best left to the reader's own imagination.

Once we were aware of our situation, we dared ask those in striped uniforms who spoke Yiddish, we wanted to know what happened to all the stuff we left behind in the wagon. They told us that all went to Canada. In our ignorance we had no clue that Canada was not the country of Canada, but the name for the warehouses the huge warehouses were the contents of all the luggage and bundles from each transport were sorted out and inventoried.

Hungarian Jews upon arrival in Auschwitz-Birkenau Death camp 1944. After two days and two nights in boxcars without food or water they are docile and relieved. They are guided by German officers and inmates in striped uniforms. The inmates are facilitators and interpreters. These man and women, hoping for the best; have no idea of the fate that is awaiting them.

Hungarian Jews after arrival in Auschwitz-Birkenau Death camp. Women and children, now separated from the men, are standing waiting for instructions. One facilitator, in striped uniform, is on the right. This picture does not portray the awful urgency and truth. Without exaggeration their next walk is to the gas chambers.

Chapter 4

HARDSHIP IN THE CAMPS

It was early morning of the next day when they marched us to Birkenau, a subsection of Auschwitz. In groups of about 100 or more, we were placed in a fenced in area each with a long barrack. Through the wire fence I could see many similar enclosed areas with people wearing the same striped uniforms.

The Kapo of our barrack was a German Gypsy (Roma), one of the few who had survived there. He was the one who told us that the Gypsies of Europe, by the thousands were brought to Birkenau a few years earlier and over time most died from starvation and disease.

The barrack had an entrance at each end. The long way through the middle was a trough, and on either side the barrack floor was bare. Those structures looked like horse stables.

After a night of horrors I was exhausted and not fully aware of our new situation. During the day we were not allowed to go inside the barrack. Around midday the meal for the day was brought in by Gypsies; most had open sores on their arms and legs. The meal called "durgemuze" came in barrels formerly oil drums; a thick soup with a rotten smell and very bitter taste. The main ingredients were beets and turnips grown as feed for livestock. Since we had no plates, we were given night potties they had unloaded from arriving transports. We gathered around the barrel, a pot was dipped into the barrel, then passed on from mouth to mouth.

At first I did not eat, I could not stand the awful putrid smell of that thick soup. Regardless of how foul the food may be, my father persuaded me that to live I had to eat. I learned to close my nostrils with my fingers, that way the swallowing part was tolerable. The fact that to the Germans we were no better than animals, and to be so quickly dehumanized was very painful. Then I started to eat everything that was given.

I willed myself to survive one day at the time, and maybe someday I'd be a witness and tell the world, so that the Nazis may be punished.

In the few weeks since we were snatched from our homes I learned to endure hardships never before imagined. From early morning we had to stay outside the barrack. When it rained to stay warm, we huddled closely together like beasts in a pasture. Even that was forbidden. SS men came often and singled out a few to punish. Some to be beaten with hard rubber clubs, others were forced to do push-ups until they dropped in the mud.

Inside the barrack the nights were torturous. We had to sit on the floor, tightly squeezed in each other's crotch. The nights were long and painful. The outhouse was at one far end outside the barrack. To leave my place I had to step over and on top of others. When I returned I could not find my spot. For my father with his hernia to sit in that position all night was very painful. Since we sat together I tried to give him as much space as I could. One night I desperately had to go to that awful outhouse. Sitting on that filthy board covered with human waist . . . I could only imagine how many thousands before me sat there on that board in fear, with stanch all around and from below. The outhouse was a big long hole in the ground, for walls on three sides wooden planks. Sitting there I looked up and saw the little dipper shine brightly in the sky above. I was always fascinated by the configuration of those stars. Back home when I used to walk on this narrow street with a starry sky above, I always saw the Little Dipper. It was unthinkable to imagine then, that at any time in my life I would be observing the little dipper from an outhouse in a prison camp at Auschwitz. Staring at the stars had a calming effect, as if to tell me "You're not lost, we'll always guide you."

The days were long and idle, we had no shelter from the sun or rain. I was in constant fear of being beaten like many others for no reason at all. A Godforsaken gloomy place, without hope, no trees, not even a blade of grass grew there. The barrack, the gravel around it, the high wire fences that separated endless enclosures like ours.

In a few days I became so hungry I would have eaten anything. I could hardly wait for the once a day soup. When the awful soup arrived we gathered around the barrel, the potty was dipped into the barrel then passed on from mouth to mouth. After a few days everybody was starving; men began to count the number of times one swallowed before the potty was passed on to the next; If one swallowed more times than agreed on, he was not allowed to eat when his turn came around again. It became perfectly clear to me the Nazis succeeded; it didn't take long to become dehumanized.

The routine was the same every day, looking through the fences in search of a recognizable face, then the only meal of the day at noontime brought out the worst in us. When it rained we huddled closely together to stay warm, and if the sun was bright and hot, a shaded spot was impossible to find. Sitting on the ground, leaning against the barrack, my father and I had very few words left to say, our thoughts were well known to each other. I didn't dare ask about my mother and the others, I wondered where my brother Bumi might be? I was glad he was not with us there. Who knows, he might be lucky enough to have escaped from being shipped off to Auschwitz.

I remembered my grandmother who loved to cook for herself. Other than Friday evening and holiday meals when she was at our table, she seldom used a plate, she ate directly from the pot. How my father used to tease her about her habit saying, that she eats from the pot so no one could see how much she ate. On occasion she was irritated by his comment. Then Rifku my sister, how is she managing by herself, she's so frail she cried so much in the cattle car on the way to Auschwitz. My mother, the last time I saw her, was holding a baby in her arms. Had she not been kind and helpful to that young mother with the two babies she might have survived the selection process and for what, to live another day, a week . . . to suffer cruelties never known before. When did those Nazis become so hateful? In all of mankind's history, man never devised and practiced such demonic tortures, and this was just the beginning; what was waiting for us we couldn't imagine.

It had been only a couple of days since we were separated yet they seemed so distant. I was afraid of the truth. Everything around us was so unreal (surreal), I felt as if we were suspended in time, time in the normal sense did not exist. As if in a terrible nightmare, I tried to understand where I was and why? I was lost.

The only hopeful information came from the Gypsy Kapo the leader of the barrack who informed us that we wouldn't be there for long.

After about ten days, that seemed like ten weeks. We marched out of there onto a train, this time a regular passenger train. While in Auschwitz or Birkenau, anything could have happened to us; evidently the Nazis needed some of us alive, for what purpose we had no idea.

After Auschwitz, stripped of identity and self worth, desperate and hopelessly forsaken, we were as docile as stunned animals taken to the slaughterhouse. My existence was of no importance to anyone except my father.

Since I was a child I was prone to headaches. I remembered when my grandmother dropped hot coals in a glass of water, her whispered words magically made my headache go away. I truly believed then that she could dispel evil from hurting me. Now, just a few days before, my grandmother's spirit and her magical words went up to heaven through a crematorium chimney in Auschwitz. I had a very bad headache. If I could only make the noise in my head go away, not hear the constant clatter of the iron wheels against the rail tracks. With each added thud our arrival, to where? Came closer and closer. I grew up knowing that my father could and would protect me from harm, in his presence I was always safe. Now we were all doomed. I was so afraid, in despair I hugged my father.

Traveling westward, the names of the towns along the way were Slavic. The sound of the whistle from a steam locomotive is the same everywhere. The cattle car train to Auschwitz also had a steam locomotive. Like an unending scream, I still remember the eerie, ghostly, long wailing whistle.

The train did not go through Hungary, it stopped once or twice to take on water for the locomotive. We traveled through Austrian towns, then past Vienna, going west. After a few hours, the train came to a screeching stop in the middle of nowhere.

I knew we were somewhere in Austria but I had no idea how far we had come. We were ordered to jump off the train and line up linking arms five in a row. Because of his hernia my father could not jump off fast enough, a guard hit him with the butt of his rifle. My father fell and rolled down over the crushed stones by the tracks. He was dazed and in pain.

The blow was unexpected, we did not see the guard who was in back of us. As I've often noted, the Germans were unnecessarily cruel all the time. This time not being sure the guard may have been Austrian.

We began our march, we left the train tracks and followed a narrow trail through a forest of young trees. It was late in the afternoon; I remember looking into the bright sun that was low on the horizon. Other than the sound of gravel under our feet, there were no other sounds, not even from the guards who were marching along both sides of the column.

A strange sensation, a fear I had not felt before came over me.

I gripped my father's hand tightly, I looked into his eyes and he too stared at me. Frightful thoughts crossed my mind, stories I had heard about how the Nazis rounded up Jews in the villages of Lithuania, and how they took them out into a forest, then shot and killed them all. For our number there appeared to be far too many armed soldiers. I could not control my fear, my chest began to pound so hard I could hardly breathe. Anticipating the worst, we just kept on walking without saying a word to each other. When we reached the end of the forest, the sun was about to fall below the horizon.

In the distance I saw a huge fortress-like structure. As we marched closer the narrow trail began to widen and it became obvious that we were marching towards the fortress. It was just like in a movie I had seen once; how the Romans or the Persians, marched their prisoners into captivity.

Sadly, that was not a make-believe scripted film, it was reality and it was happening to us. What a walking, living nightmare; to endure I needed all the courage I could gather.

The gate was wide open, row after row we marched inside the belly of the fortress beast. The reception was predictable, the fierce look in the German guards' eyes pierced like arrows.

In a short few weeks I learned to accept that we were not on trial, good behavior would not change our fate, we were all condemned to die, but not to know when or by what means,

Once inside the fortress, my fears changed to a new reality. The will to live grew in proportion to the dangers perceived or real. I was grateful having lived through another day.

MAUTHAUSEN

This prison fortress was the main concentration camp in Austria. From there many thousands of prisoners were sent to other labor camps all over Austria. For me, date of month or time of day lost meaning. The only important thing was to save as much energy as possible, avoid getting beaten, survive one day at a time, and most importantly, remain sane. So far we were spared from having numbers tattooed on our arms.

In Mauthausen I received an inmate number with a yellow triangle painted on a strip of cloth and fastened to my striped jacket. My father's number was 75126, my number was 75128. Our clothes consisted of a shirt with long underpants made of a light gray fabric; jacket, pants and cap of a similar fabric with vertical blue stripes. Every time we moved from one place to another the mix of people changed, some from Poland some Czech and most from Hungary. I have never been with Jews or non Jews from so many different countries in one place before.

Our daily routine was the same as in Birkenau; except each compound was surrounded by high stonewalls.

We spent the days outside the barrack, and we could only enter for the night. Instead of sitting in each other's crotch as we did in Birkenau, for the night here we had to lie on one side, like fish in a barrel. Once we lay down we were set for the night. It was impossible to turn around in place. For fear of getting clubbed by the night Kapo my father and I didn't dare move or leave our place. Our daily rations were minimal.

The stone walls that framed the compound were about ten feet or higher; in bright daylight not even birds flew over the fortress, the sun never reached us below, it felt like being in a dungeon. Each compound held fewer people than in Birkenau. Here some brothers were separated, some fathers were also separated from their sons. Fortunately my father and I were still together. In Mauthausen also I was in constant fear, often people were taken out for no cause and didn't come back. After about four or five days maybe a week, as part of a large transport, we were sent to Melk. For better or for worse I was much relieved and so was my father when we left.

The train ride from Mauthausen to Melk was short and uneventful. The train station in Melk was a typical Austrian small town station. As we marched past the outside of the ticket office and waiting room, I could not help but notice the propaganda posters on the wall. One warned the populace to be aware of spies, "Pst!! Der Find Hert Mit" (beware the enemy listens). Another poster simply stated in large capitol letters "DIE JUDEN SIND UNSER UMGLUCK" (the Jews are our misfortune) those hateful Nazi propaganda images; any rational person could see the vicious distortion of fact perpetrated by the Nazis.

MELK

Before it was turned into a concentration camp, Melk was a German (Austrian) military or some kind of police garrison located in this old picturesque town with a 900 plus year old monastery with the Danube River flowing in-between. The camp was located on high ground, with a good view of the surrounding area. When we arrived, the camp already had a large inmate population of many nationalities from all over Europe.

We were housed in brick buildings and many wooden barracks, all surrounded by an electrified chain-link fence and guard towers with mounted machine guns. The infirmary was in a wooden barrack right next to block # 5, and off the center of the camp there was a small diving pool. The German officers and guards were housed in red brick buildings near the main gate on the other side of the electrified fence.

My father and I were assigned to block #5, a red brick building with two floors. Large rooms branched out on either side of the center staircase. We were assigned to a second floor room. The room was long and wide with rows of two tier wooden bunk beds. The opposite wall had glass paneled windows with iron grates. Standing at the window I could see the guard towers and into the distance far below, I could see a river the Danube River. Every bunk bed had a covered mattress, a pillow and a military grey blanket. My father settled in a lower bunk and I above him. For the first time we could be relieved knowing that we were brought there to work.

Housing was satisfactory, the room and bunk beds were clean; the ever present fear left me somewhat and we waited for what came next. Shortly after that afternoon, a Kapo came into the room and told us to go down for general roll call; that was to be our first roll call in Melk. Halfway down the stairs someone called out loudly, They're taking our shoes from us" That was the only thing we had that was ours, brought from home. In desperation we ran back to our room, took off our good shoes, and hid them under the mattresses. On the way to the Appel-Platz I stepped into water puddles. By the time we lined up for the appel, (roll call) my bare feet were convincingly muddy and dirty. My father did the same; the practice was, that if you had no shoes, you were given a pair. The standard camp shoe was a wooden clog with a few straps stapled to it, very uncomfortable and difficult to walk in. If you showed up with decent shoes, Kapos forced you to take them off, they kept them for themselves, and gave you a pair of camp shoes. After my father and I returned to the room we learned that others also saved their shoes that way.

During the night all shoes had to be placed in front of each bunk bed; we kept our good shoes hidden, instead we displayed the wooden clogs we were given. Most of the German Kapos were condemned criminals serving long sentences. They were the willing executors of every Nazi command. Each block had a leader in charge, a Block Fuhrer and an assistant to the leader. At times they were self-appointed, nobody cared except when they enjoyed privileges, extra food or easier work assignments.

As the day progressed the Kapos told us that our work will be in Shachtbau, (tunnel construction). The entire labor force was divided into three shifts; morning, afternoon and night shifts; alternating each week. For breakfast we had a piece of bread, a small cube of margarine, a piece of sausage and coffee. For the main meal of the day we had a thick vegetable soup and bread. The soup was not as bad as in Birkenau. We each had a metal spoon and an enameled metal soup bowl, so as not to lose it, we punched a small hole near the rim through which we pulled a string or a piece of wire and tied the plate to a button hole in the jacket. Observing others we learned what to do. Wherever we went the soup bowl went with us.

Before we left the camp for work, we had to line up at the Appel-Platz, there the Kapos and block Fuhrers counted heads, and reported our numbers to the military commander. If all were present we were allowed to leave the camp. If someone was missing, a search began, no one was permitted to leave until the person or missing persons were found. The obsession with numbers was severe. Sometimes the missing person was found in his bunk bed or the outhouse, very sick and unable to walk. The heftling (inmate) was usually found by a Kapo and by the time he was dragged out to the Appel-Platz he was beaten so badly he seldom survived the day.

After all were accounted for, dead or alive, we were allowed to leave the camp. Outside the gate the guards armed with rifles joined the march. They positioned themselves on both sides of the column.

On rainy days the guards wore raincoats and gloves, we wore only the striped clothes we were given. After about half an hour we reached a long platform that was built along the rail tracks just for our use. There we waited for the train that took us to Schachtbau, (tunnel construction) the work site was outside the village of Rogendorf, a village along a sandstone mountain; about 2 Km. From the famous Abbey in the town of Melk. On the first day, we were divided into groups, and then taken to different workstations along the side of the mountain. Entrances to three or four tunnels were in the early stages of construction.

Now my father's main concern was to find a way he could improvise a device to support his hernia. He managed to find a piece of hard cardboard that he shaped to fit the area. I really don't remember how, but he managed to tie that device around his lower abdomen. His hernia slipped out sometimes but he managed to get it back into place.

There was no shortage of slave man power. To dislodge the sandstone we used explosives, compressed air powered boring equipment and highly mechanized boring machines the size of a small tank that advanced on it's own chain rails. The boring part had many cutting blades shaped like blades on a huge fan. Those sharp blades cut through the sandstone wall, then automatically gathered and pushed the excavated sandstone material to the rear of the machine. All we had to do was to shovel the sand onto the nearest conveyor belt that carried the material outside the tunnel. In other offshoots from the main tunnel we bored through the sandstone with long sharp pointed iron drills attached to hand held jack hammers. Young boys, fourteen or fifteen years old, were the Spitzen Trager (drill carriers). The iron drills had to be sharpened often. The boys carried the sharp drills to the workstations, and then took the dulled drills back to the blacksmith to be resharpened. For young boys, it was very hard work to carry those heavy iron drills back and forth. The dislodged sandstone we then shoveled onto conveyor belts, which looked like black rivers flowing from the tunnels. To prevent cave-ins, the overhead had to be shored up with lumber.

Whole forests must have been cut down for that purpose. Eventually we dug the tunnels deeper and deeper into the mountain.

The area of the project spread out for at least a kilometer in length. During the summer months, working outside the tunnels, exposed to the hot sun, without safe drinking water was very hard. Many who could not hold out drank water that was polluted or had harmful chemicals in it. Some of the Foremen if asked, did point out places where the water was safer to drink. It always appeared to me that more people were working there than had come from our camp. There may have been others from other nearby labor camps. I seldom dared to go beyond my work station. Then for some weeks we worked inside the tunnel. First we advanced a few meters then we drilled holes overhead in opposite sides of the tunnel walls, then we slid the supporting lumber into the holes. To prevent the sandstone ceiling from falling down on us, we then forced in long wood shingle slats packed tightly above the parallel supporting lumber. Other times we worked outside the tunnel carrying lumber, cement bags or shoveling sandstone on the conveyor belts. We did everything.

The capo of our room in block 5, was Breiner, his father-in-law about 60 years old, and Klein a cousin or friend of Breiner, and the hospital orderly and a few others had all come from a town near Budapest. Occasionally there was friction and resentment toward Breiner. Frequently he assigned easier tasks to his compatriots, a bunk bed away from near the entrance, or favored his friends with leftover soup or coffee. There was also much trading in foodstuffs, soup for bread, a portion of margarine and sausage for bread; even articles of clothing were traded. I never traded anything, I was content with what I had. I ate my rations as given; when I saved a piece of bread in my pocket it turned into crumbs. Our bread was made from very little grain flour, mostly sawdust. My father and I had our meals together, with tin plates in hand we stood in long lines in front of our block. The afternoon meal was soup and bread, for breakfast we had coffee, bread, a small piece of margarine and a piece of wurst (sausage).

My father once said can you believe it, this sausage tastes so good, look what we have missed in our kosher foods. Not that we didn't have cold cuts or processed meats at home; we were strictly Kosher. My mother seldom bought salami or other kinds of precooked processed foods.

I also think my father must have remembered the kinds of meat products that were part of his diet during his service in the Austro-Hungarian Army in WW I. My father and I were able to adjust to the day by day challenges. Work was hard; if we dared to rest for a minute the Kapos with their hard rubber clubs were all over us, but just being together was comforting. The daily rations were never enough, they always left us hungry. My father was 56 years old, he worked side by side with younger men. He never asked for any consideration. Although his hernia bothered him, he never complained about it. So far we had no problems inside or outside the camp. We helped and looked out for each other in every way.

Then something happened, it came as a surprise somehow we were separated. We were no longer in the same shift but were still in the same block in the same room, except that he was placed on the morning shift. When his shift was coming in from work, mine was preparing to go out but, we still saw each other once a day. It had only been a couple of days and I missed not being with him. Everything was so much easier to endure together.

On a warm sunny day in July, we had about half an hour before we had to assemble on the appel platz. While others were outside picking lice off their shirts (a time well spent), I decided to spend the remaining time in the room where it was cool and more comfortable resting on my bunk bed. Then I was startled by the loud sound of the air raid siren. I jumped up and looked out the window. To my disbelief I saw bombs fall out of the sky and watched them explode as they fell in the field. I crawled under the table along the wall for safety. After several more explosions, one after the other, the glass windows blew in, the bunk beds, mattresses, blankets and pillows were all over the room. The few of us there feared the building might collapse.

Dr. Wolf a fellow inmate, grabbed my hand and together we ran down the stairs. The entrance to our block was already jammed with those who ran inside the building for cover. We managed to get out, and away from the building. Bombs that fell inside the camp made large craters in the ground. The two of us jumped into a crater. At that moment we thought it was the safest place to be.

Then I saw two planes pass overhead. The bombing had stopped, but the strafing continued. They were shooting at everything that moved. While in the crater the planes passed over us twice. Bullets were flying all around us but Dr. Wolf and I were not hit. After it was all over I came out of the crater unharmed, only with a small scratch on my right wrist.

In spite of the air attack, not one building or barrack was hit. When the bombing began, the safest place was out in the open we thought, but the machine gun fire from the attacking airplanes turned the camp into a battlefield with wounded lying all over on the ground.

Hundreds were injured; many died most horrible deaths. We tried to help the wounded but for many it was too late. I saw boys from my home town bleed to death. There was little we could do to help. One had his arm ripped from the shoulder and with his other hand held the arm that was hanging by skin alone. Wounded men were lying on the blood-soaked ground. Two brothers from a village near my hometown were on the ground, badly wounded. They comforted each other while bleeding to death. There I was with a harmless scratch on my wrist, while others were seriously wounded and dying. The water in the small pool in the middle of the camp turned a deep red from the blood of those who tried to wash their wounds.

The twins, everybody knew the twin brothers about 16-years-old, rather tall for their age, with delicate features and flaming red hair. When bread rations were handed out they held it in their hands, looking at the piece of bread as if not knowing what to do with it, eat it or save it for later. One time while standing and contemplating what to do, a fellow inmate snatched it out of ones hands and disappeared in the crowd. After the bombing I never saw the twins again.

Many boys from my hometown were killed that day. Among them was the boy whose inmate number was 75127, the number between my father's and mine.

I can't remember the names of the many who died that day but their faces and agony are deeply carved into my memory. Those images are still with me; I will never forget that day as long as I live.

My shift did not leave the camp for work that day, instead the entire camp was involved with the cleanup. Every block and every barrack had many casualties. First we helped take the wounded to the hospital, then we removed the dead; most of the seriously wounded did not survive.

The small infirmary could not care for all. The hospital staff was also inmates, they tried their best to care for the injured. The Nazis were not interested in healing anyone.

Hours later when my father's shift returned from shachtbau (tunnel work), he was horrified by what he saw and was desperate to find me. It was late afternoon before we found each other.

Who bombed us and why? We never found out. The Germans probably knew; speculation was that the planes were British and mistook the target for a German army camp. Since the war in Vietnam and other military conflicts, such losses in human life were called, "Killed by friendly fire"

On that Saturday morning at 5 minutes before 11 the camp clock stopped.

From then on our situation worsened. The small hospital was full with the sick and wounded; poor sanitation and malnutrition became a major cause for disease and death.

Hunger, starvation and exhaustion were killing us rapidly. It became very hard to hold on to the smallest measure of hope. We were so weak we no longer washed ourselves. In the morning we were still so exhausted we would rest in bed a few extra minutes rather than go to the washroom.

We began to be infested with lice. Little creatures, the size of small grains of wheat, hid inside the seams and stitches of our clothes. A small piece of bread I had saved in my pocket, to my horror was crawling with lice. With great care I removed the lice, then ate the bread crumbs.

Every day was the same; with small variations some days were worse then others. Melk was not Auschwitz or MAUTHAUSEN, it was the end of the line of possibilities. In less than two months from living in relative freedom in Besztercze; compared to how Jews were treated, mistreated in other parts of Europe. In Polish Ghettoes were degradation took months, in some places years before deportation to Auschwitz and other death camps. That sudden uprooting from our homes to a hillside a few Km, outside of our town in one day, that cruel act against us was so paralyzing, that all previous predictions, forewarnings, calculations, miscalculations, none mattered.

There were individuals who prepared themselves they planned for this eventuality, some had brought with them money, jewels, hidden in their clothes, all such calculations, possibilities were useless. This enemy was unimaginably brutal. In other times, other places, to bribe an official, a guard, a hijacker, was an accepted norm. This brutal enemy wanted, and took all. First he took our material possessions, then, our present, past and future, we were to be eliminated without a trace of ever having existed; and our compatriot and neighbors collaborated knowingly or unknowingly as the case may have been, with the Nazis or Fascists of the time. All that false security was gone. After surviving the selection process in Auschwitz/Birkenau and after Mauthausen, and now in Melk, all thoughts about what could have or should have been done, nothing mattered anymore. The stark reality of the moment was so devastating as if waking from a nightmare, but being awake was far worse than the dream.

On July 21, the attempted assassination of Hitler had failed. We had no reliable account of the event, except some German civilians at the work site had spread the news. At first we believed that the assassination was successful, but we soon heard that Hitler was not harmed. Even though the conference room was blown up, the explosion did kill others but it did not harm Hitler. The hope of an early end to the war was again shattered, and that also added to our misery.

The crematorium in Melk had been under construction, until it was finished the dead were shipped to Mauthausen daily, or some other place to be cremated. A dysentery epidemic broke out and my father also came down with it. Those with the symptoms, including my father, were isolated from the others. My father was taken to a special ward in the hospital barrack next to our block.

Added to the hundreds who died from hunger and abusive treatment, many more died each day from this dreaded disease. It was attributed to drinking polluted and contaminated water. The treatment was starvation, and to reverse dehydration, the sick were given boiled water and weak watered-down coffee once a day.

The treatment seemed to help. I knew the hospital orderly who made frequent visits to our room. I wish I remembered his name, he was very kind and helpful to my father. He was from a town near Budapest, his friend was Breiner the schtuben fuhrer, and his buddy Klein who seemed to be running things, and they were secretive, projecting an air of importance about themselves. To me their behavior was more comical than practical.

The hospital orderly came to see them almost daily, and to inform me about my father's condition. According to his account the sickness ran its course for a week or two. The difficulty was to survive that week. Not to drink tap water was a must, he also told me that my father needed additional safe liquids. They didn't have enough sterilized or boiled liquids to satisfy the burning thirst of all the sick.

My father's bunk bed was next to a window that faced directly onto the yard. A wire fence and a patch of green grass separated us.

I saved my coffee in a corked bottle, a bottle I obtained from a civilian foreman at work. In the afternoon after I returned from work, when the yard was crowded with people, I went to the fence facing my father's window as close as I could, and slid the bottle on the grass until it hit the fence. From there the friendly orderly took the bottle to my father, I waited until my father held up the bottle and showed it to me. The exchange went on smoothly for some days. I was in constant fear that I might lose him. Every day I returned from work not knowing whether he'd still be alive. Many were dying every day. Under those conditions it was almost impossible to recover. The supervisor at the work site who gave me the empty bottle, he knew why I needed it I had informed him about my father's condition. He always wanted to know if my father was getting better. I never thought to ask him to bring coffee himself in that bottle for me.

One night, at the beginning of the shift, the same supervisor gave me two apples and an onion. It was so kind of him to do that. I was so happy to receive the fruit. I wanted so much to eat one apple and bring the other back to camp for my father. Knowing how happy he would be, I successfully resisted the temptation. I fondled an apple in my pocket all night but did not bite into it. I could hardly wait for the shift to end and return to the camp.

After getting back from work we usually were allowed to disperse right away and go to our barracks, but this time we were kept on the appel platz. In a short while SS officers came through the gate and began a body search of all who had just returned from work. What they were looking for really didn't seem to matter. It was one of those unpredictable times; just to harass and torment us. We were ordered to remove everything from our pockets, put the contents in our caps and present the caps for inspection. The search was slow and methodical. Some of us were searched more thoroughly than others.

From a distance I could see that some were allowed to leave, while others were condemned to be whipped. A few SS officers, with long oxtail whips the weapon of choice, began to beat them. The inmates were held down over a wooden horse, while an SS officer was striking without mercy, the other counted the lashes.

As the punishment was in progress, the condemned had to wait in line for their turn to be beaten. I already had emptied my pockets into my cap, I had nothing other than the two apples and the onion.

I was scared to death. I threw the apples away, the onion I put back in my pants pocket, and just stood there waiting for my turn. The SS officer looked into my empty cap, then pointing with his long stick shouted, "What is that in your pocket?" Meekly I showed him the onion. Angrily he knocked the onion out of my hand with his stick, then ordered me to stand in line to be whipped.

That line had grown rapidly. Those who had been whipped could not walk away on their own, one at the time they were dragged away onto a pile. I was in mortal fear. I could see those who had been beaten were in terrible agony. Way ahead of the line I saw SS men, all very busy, one counting the lashes, the other with the whip, in rolled-up shirt sleeves, shouting their usual curses, perspiring heavily.

Risking a terrible beating I made a split second decision; I walked over and threw myself on the pile of those who had already been whipped. There I lay without moving, hoping desperately that no one had observed me. I lay there on top of the others for some time. People around me were crying in pain. After the SS had finished their brutal game they left the camp.

Later that day when the shock wore off a little, I told a roommate about the apples, the onion and the chance I took to avoid a beating. I also wanted to let my father know what I had brought for him and lost, but decided against it. He had enough to worry about.

A few days later, one late afternoon after roll call, the friendly hospital orderly came to tell me that my father wanted to see me that evening, it was very urgent and that he, the orderly, would arrange the place where we could meet. Later that evening my father came through the alley between the two buildings. I could see his shadow as he came towards the fence that separated us. It was the first time in two weeks that we saw each other close. We began to cry. He looked very frail, he had lost so much weight; I wanted to stop crying but couldn't.

My father began by telling about the difficult choice he had to make. He was told that he was considered cured, not contagious anymore, and would be discharged that night. He would be sent out to work with the night shift, or he could go to Mauthausen, with an exchange transport next morning. By choosing to leave for Mauthausen he hoped to get some time to regain his strength. All he hoped for was to be able to rest a few more days in the infirmary but since the infirmary was crowded they would not let him stay. We both felt that in his condition, working underground in the tunnels, he could not survive even one night.

That exchange option had not been offered before. The crematorium in Melk was under construction. Up to that point, only the dead were sent to Mauthausen and, in exchange about 800 to 1000 fresh prisoners were sent to Melk each month. It was the most difficult decision we had to make. "What should I do? What should I do? He kept saying, he couldn't decide. I really didn't know what to do what to say, I wanted him to stay, but I also was afraid, seeing how frail he was I was scared, I felt that this was a decision he had to make. After much soul-searching my father decided to take a chance and go to Mauthausen. We touched hands, we kissed through the wire fence, and we parted never to see each other again.

The night we separated, the moment we parted I'll never forget. Had he stayed with me, would he have had a better chance to survive? Did he choose to leave thinking that by leaving it would be easier for me? I have not forgiven myself for agreeing to the separation.

What if I had protested and pleaded with him to stay? Why was I not more persuasive? What was on his mind? How could I have agreed with such a choice? My father was 56 years old; before he became ill he was a healthy strong man. He worked as hard as anyone else. After so many years, the memory of that night is still very painful.

I cannot forgive the Germans for their deliberate cruelty, to reduce us to an existence where such choices had to be made. We worked so hard but they did not care about us one way or the other, whether we lived or perished. They delighted in seeing us squirm for a piece of bread. They never failed to be cruel; at times when we scraped the crusted leftovers from inside the barrels, the Nazi officers made sport laughing, chasing and beating us with their whips. I never understood how these young officers could behave that way. I often wondered how they could live with themselves, how could they sleep at night.

While my father was in the so called hospital I looked forward to exchange glances with him through the window from a distance; The next day I missed him terribly, I began to feel guilty and depressed.

Sometime in August a transport of about two hundred Greek prisoners arrived. I had never seen Greek men other than in pictures before. They looked so different, on average they were short, dark-haired, with pale olive skin complexions. They were gentle people, they could have been prisoners of war. They did not speak or understand German, and were more vulnerable than we were. We could not communicate with them, there may or may not have been Jews among them. Maybe they were all Jewish. Greek Jews don't speak Yiddish, I did not know that then. When the cold icy rains came, most of them died from exposure to a climate they were not used to.

The fall weather was harsh it rained a lot. Our skimpy striped uniforms did not shield us from the cold rain and wind. Day after day, the down hill march to the ramp, and the waiting for the train that took us to the work site and back, and the endless roll calls were exhausting and depressing.

The work load became harder each day. We dug the tunnels deeper, wider and higher; we used hundreds of tree trunks to shore up the walls and ceilings, and we mixed tons of cement then hoisted it all onto the scaffolds. On the surface the walls looked solid, but tremors from explosives and compressed air powered jacks caused ceilings to fall, burying those who worked underneath. When a section of the tunnel was wide and high enough we built scaffolds to support the frames for pouring concrete. With time, whatever our task was, it became more difficult to do. We lifted tree trunks off the ground and placed them in the pre-bored holes in the wall. What two or four men used to do, now took six or eight of us, and with much difficulty.

When I worked on the second or third layer of the tunnel, it was very dangerous. The lower ceilings used to give way and collapse.

I escaped a few near-misses. Other times I was fortunate to work deep in the tunnel on a first level of excavation. On night shifts deep underground there were fewer supervisors on location. We took advantage, on many occasions we tied the jackhammer's trigger with a piece of wire and laid it flat on the ground. The grinding noise continued; that way we could rest for a while. Besides compressed air powered jackhammers we used dynamite to dislodge the sandstone. The mining engineers taught us how to light long fuses and how to hide from the impact of the explosions. Working with dynamite was relatively safe, working on the scaffolds was dangerous. Because of inadequate support the scaffolds collapsed, bringing down many to their deaths. Life was cheap and slave labor was plentiful.

Remembering those days, it seems to me that the Nazis learned their cruelties by practice. Each transport, with carloads of Jews, gave them fresh material to practice with, and perfect their trade in becoming the world's mass killers.

For over fifty years' philosophers, historians have been searching to understand the Holocaust, as if the Holocaust had followed some precise formula. This Nazi cancer evolved predictably to one end, to murder millions, including non Jews who did not measure up to their perceived Aryan model.

There are those who think that Nazi programs had been predetermined not only with end result, but also step by step as some choreographed program. With hindsight we can all say that yes, once we were in their hands we were all condemned to die. Where, how, and by what means and when, was left to chance.

On arrival to Auschwitz did we know what kind of place that was? Of course not. The question that should be asked; after the selection process, how did we manage to survive? I think we survived not because we were physically strong, resourceful, or clever; those attributes may have helped. For example the *Sonder-Commando*, a special group of inmates, who upon the arrival of each train transport to Auschwitz were the first to jump inside the wagons. They encouraged the people to leave everything behind. In all the archival photographs that show a mass of bewildered people, you can see among them men in striped uniforms, who were the facilitators who calmed the newcomers, some guided the condemned men, women and children to the gas chambers, some also worked the crematoriums. They were a select group who enjoyed better treatment. Their privileges came with a terrible price. Every four or five weeks they also were done away with. That information became known to us much later in the year of 1944.

With hindsight not all KZ lagers were the same, depending on the type of labor we were subjected to: In some camps housing was better than in others. In some camps medical experiments on inmates was extensive, in others not at all. Hunger, skimpy clothing, wooden clogs for shoes, and terrible cold in winter. Whatever we wore seldom got a chance to dry, our clothes dried on our backs if at all. Dirty, infested with lice and always desperately hungry, our numbers fell. In Melk out of an average camp population of 8000, up to 1000 of us died every month. With every passing month, less and less of a chance to survive. In other camps I've been told the situation was even worse. Yes, we were all condemned to die, we were never to be released for good behavior. In spite of all that, we worked, we suffered, and we struggled for that one chance against all odds to stay alive.

Rosh Hashanah

On average I did not know what day of the week it was; it made no difference to me, Monday or Friday, every day was the same. I was very depressed. This was the first Rosh Hashanah that I was separated from my family. On holidays my brother, my father and I were always together in the synagogue. In my room there were a few very religious men. They observed the Sabbath and Holidays, it was remarkable to see their transformation in prayer. Without prayer books or any ritual objects, they recited by heart and prayed with absolute faith in the Almighty. Men I had known from back home, who had beards with long side-locks, now with shorn heads, stood straight facing Eastward and prayed. I also stood up and joined them in prayer.

The solemnity of the day was in our prayers . . . (From selected Psalms translated from the Hebrew text)

"Out of the depth have I cried to the Lord,
He answered me and set me free.
You have heard my plea,
Do not turn away from my prayers.
Be my protector"

Our prayer leader chose the next verses, in Hebrew of course. Legend has it that this prayer was first uttered by a martyred Rabbi Amnon who was mutilated for refusing to give up his faith. The poet Kalonymos of Mayence, of the eleventh century composed the prayer in its present form.

UNSANE TOKEF

"Let us declare the mighty holiness of this day, on this day it is written;
Who shall live and who shall die,
Who shall die by fire and who by water,
Who by famine, and who by thirst,
Who by strangling and who by stonening,
Who shall be at rest and who shall wander,
Who shall be humbled and who shall be exalted."

Every year on high holy days we recited those verses, but never before had they been so heartfelt. The utterance of every word had the weight of centuries of Jewish prayer and believe in God.

To end the short prayer, standing between the bunk beds we recited the "Mourners Kadish" a prayer a son is obligated to recite for a departed parent. We were all sons of fathers and fathers of sons, living in the valley of the shadow of death, dying of hunger and by other cruel means.

We prayed to the "Almighty" the God of our fathers, who for some mysterious reason was not counting us among the living any more.

"He" abandoned us to the Nazis; should we all die here, no one will remember that we ever existed. To the Nazis we were just numbers; people without names, without value as human beings. The chances of survival were very slim. There were many among us who said it is not worth suffering and struggling, others said we must prove to the world that we existed, unless some of us survive, to bear witness how will anyone know what these Nazi murderers did.

As I write and remember those moments, I find myself asking the same questions over and over. Why did all those horrible things happen to us? Does faith and belief in God make any difference? Does prayer really matter? Does The God who created the universe play chance with human life? Is one human life worth less than another? We did not pray to be saved from Genocide; that word was not in use, or it's idea understood.

On Yom-Kipur (the day of atonement) we acknowledge our sins, as a community we pray for forgiveness, for past and present sins, we pray for a life free from sickness, and free from mental anguish, we pray to be spared from natural disasters; fire, floods and the plague, (witch were considered punishment by God) we prayed to the God of our fathers to save us, as a father cares for his children and the children of all mankind.

Our past and present teachers thought us that man was created in God's image. Not in the physical sense but with God like attributes. I need not remind the reader, it is common knowledge that the best and the brightest of our people were destroyed, murdered during the Nazi years in Europe. The greatest minds among the Jewish people, among others, were turned into ashes. I can still hear my mother's voice before we arrived to Auschwitz. Her last words were to remind God not to allow such bad things happen to us. She still believed in common human decency that people don't do heartless things to others.

Of those religious men I prayed with on that Rosh Hashanah and Yom-Kipur day, not one survived. With regularity, one by one, day by day, overworked and starved, they all perished under the most inhuman conditions. Who is saying Kadish for them, who are remembering them now?

From the forehead to the back of the neck a wide strip had been shaven off our heads. In case of escape a prisoner could not hide and would easily be recognized and eventually recaptured. On a few occasions there were attempted escapes.

At roll call when the count was short, we all suffered. On such occasions we had to stay on the appel-platz (roll cal) until the missing person or persons were accounted for. I remember when a Ukrainian fellow escaped. On a return march from work he ran out of the column. Armed soldiers with dogs chased after him in the nearby woods. He was captured, brought back, and in front of all of us was severely beaten, and with his hands tied to his feet, he was suspended upside down and let hang from a pole. After we were dismissed, hours later into the night, he was still hanging from that pole. No one ever survived those tortures. I always admired the courage of those who attempted to escape.

Yom Kippur

Ten days after Rosh Hashanah is Yom Kippur. Traditionally a day of fasting and personal reflection. By then our shift had changed to the morning schedule. By eight in the morning the shift was out of the camp and on the way to the tunnels. We woke up before six and went to the washrooms and toilets. In half an hour we had to be washed, dressed, our bunk beds made up, and lined up for breakfast outside. That morning Instead of the usual coffee in the barrel, there was cream of wheat with milk, creamy white and hot. Since I was a young boy, I always fasted on Yom Kippur. Were it not for the religious men around me, I probably would not have known that it was Yom Kippur morning. Most did not fast, for me It became a test of will, I decided to fast but those who did not had a great breakfast with seconds. I'm sure the cream of wheat was not meant for us, that one barrel was intended probably for the German guards, but it lost its way to our block.

As the cold weather came upon us, working outside in front of the tunnels became very hard. The rain soaked sandstone dirt was heavy to shovel, it was a blessing or luck when I was assigned to work inside the tunnel. A shift underground allowed enough time for my clothes to dry. If it didn't rain while marching to and from work we considered ourselves fortunate. Hard work, freezing cold and unimaginable hunger became an everyday event.

I was reduced to a state where, all I could think of was the next meal. Would the next ladle of soup have more vegetables or will my next portion of bread be bigger? Hunger pains and fear never left me. The endless roll calls in the freezing rain, and seeing fellow inmates fall to the ground and not be able to help in any way. The Kapos imitated the Nazis, they became devoid of human feelings. The instinct to survive became a mere flicker, many committed suicide by walking into the electrified fence.

When did it happen? When did we stop having value as human beings?

When did the moment come that we dared not remember the connection to our past?

When did it happen that memory stopped being a part of our lives?

When did it happen that I stopped feeling pain? Memory of family and home became more distant every day.

To survive, new methods needed to be learned and relearned. For every crisis we had to find a new solution. On icy cold mornings I washed superficially and start the day that way. On one such morning a French inmate showed those around him how to wash oneself in winter. He bared himself to the waist, bent over the washbasin, vigorously washed, with ice-cold water running over his head and back. When he put his shirt on, steam rose from his body. I followed his example and benefited from it, for hours after, I was less cold, and we learned a useful lesson.

Also, the kind of shoes we had was very important. If you had shoes that protected your feet, you were less exposed to foot injuries. Imagine how hard it was for those who wore the wooden clogs the camp provided. Fortunately my shoes were still the same ones I left home with.

On one occasion I was caught off guard when a group of young Ukrainians inmates caught me alone in a passageway of the tunnel. They demanded I give them my shoes. I refused and tried to get away from them. They started to beat me I was knocked to the ground, and desperately fought back to protect myself; when out of nowhere an SS officer happened to pass by. As he came nearer, the Ukrainians left me alone and ran away.

The SS officer was not aware of what had happened. I was extremely lucky, I escaped a brutal beating, or even worse, the possibility of being left barefooted. Back at my work station I told my coworkers about the incident. I realized I had to do something to make my shoes less desirable.

I needed a sharp tool but we were forbidden to possess any kind of sharp objects. I found a piece of broken glass and carefully not to cut through the lining, I made several cross cuts in the front and sides of my shoes, then with pieces of wire, I sewed the slashed uppers together. My shoes were so mutilated that nobody ever looked at them again.

Out of desperate necessity we learned to make use of empty cement bags. I think everyone knows that cement for construction comes in strong paper bags that hold about 50 lb. or more of cement. This, mixed with sand and water turns into concrete. We used these bags for undergarments. At the bottom of the empty bag I made an opening that was large enough to pull over my head. I wore it under my shirt like a sleeveless vest. The paper sack shielded me from the cold wind and rain.

I still had my shoes, I had a paper vest, and so far I had learned well. As I think back on those dark days my anger rises again and again at the Nazis who treated us so brutally. The German guards knew about the paper vests, to detect if we wore them they slapped our backs at random, those with paper vests were ordered to take them off.

One night I was working outside a tunnel entrance; the sandstone that had fallen off the conveyer belt had to be shoveled on again. I had to urinate but the outhouse was at a distance and I was afraid to go there by myself. It was not wise to wander off in the dark to a place where nobody, not even the Kapo knew you. I decided to go behind the tool shed near the electrified fence. Although it was a clear night I did not see the guard tower on the other side of the fence. Suddenly I heard the click of a rifle and a loud shout "halt" I froze, I didn't move, I just looked up in that direction. The guard asked "what are you doing there?" I answered in German, I'm sorry but I urgently had to go. My answer must have amused him and he began a conversation with me. He wanted to know where I was from and where I learned to speak German. I answered his questions; I told him I had friends who were Folk Deutche, and that we always spoke German.

By then I could see his profile. He was a young soldier about my age and began to speak about himself; he had been wounded on the 'Ost' Eastern front. After his recovery he was sent to Melk to this work cite for guard duty. His voice appeared to be calm not hostile. He asked me to come closer to the fence, I hesitated, I was afraid. He told me not to fear, I should come nearer, and he wanted to give me something. Reluctantly I approached and looked up, and saw him take something out of his lunch box, which he threw down to me. I thanked him and went back to my station. He had given me half a sandwich, dark bread with two slices of 'wurst' sausage, wrapped in white paper.

Back in July, I had a similar experience. My father and I were still together, we had not been separated then. One night, after we got off the train, we marched back to the camp in rows of five, I on the outside with father on my right, and guards on both sides of the column. One guard shouted obscenities every time he walked past me. That went on for some time. Once he even pushed me with the butt of his rifle. We sensed there was something wrong, but couldn't imagine why he was picking on me. I feared what might happen if this continued. Then again I heard the guard shout the usual curses. This time when he reached my line he shoved a loaf of bread into my arms. Now I dared look at him. My father and I were very surprised. We believed the commotion that preceded the generous act was to distract the other guards' attention from himself. Those acts of kindness, although rare, I remember, and will always remember.

Day after day, hard work, hunger, and above all despair was a combination that drove many to suicide. They ran into, and grabbed the high voltage electrified fence; to die that way was very quick. I often tried to understand, what took more courage; to live under those conditions or just give up.

When we were first brought to Melk there were many fathers with sons. As time passed the fathers died, the thirteen, fourteen and fifteen year old boys were on their own; for an extra piece of bread or a plate of soup homosexual Kapos lured some of the boys. I must admit I had no clue what homosexual behavior was. I was naive about that form of sexual behavior. Even when the act was explained to me I thought it was a substitute rather then a sexual preference. I learned that there were homosexual Germans not political prisoners in camp, and since some were Kapos, I feared them without considering the cause for their incarceration.

Some time in late October, a transport of a few hundred inmates arrived from Mauthausen. To my surprise one man looked me up and brought an oral message from my father. I said oral because there was never a written communication possible. For as long I was in the camps I had no paper or pencil and saw no one else have any. My father expressed concern about my well being, he wished I could find a way to let him know about myself. My father didn't know that his transfer to Mauthausen, was a one-time exception. In July after my father left, only the dead were sent back by truck to be cremated. The crematorium in Melk was now operating, and no one left Melk, dead or alive.

Transports of men who came to Melk were replacements for those who died. About one thousand people died each month and the replacements kept on coming. They were mainly Jews, but there were also many others: Poles, Ukrainians, Russians, Czechs, French, Greeks and some Germans.

Two more messages came from my father, the last one at the end of December. Each time someone who knew where to find me came with the same message, "Your father is well and he is concerned about your well being"

My friends, the Lowy brothers, Simon and Herman, were also in Block 5; at times we worked in the same shift. They were helpful, especially Simon. He was a good role model. Simon was very different, he could turn a bad situation around. The daily hardships he considered as obstacles, and obstacles needed to be overcome. Simon and Herman also were deported from Besztercze. We were in the same ghetto, but we didn't go to Auschwitz with the same transport.

Herman was with the Nathan family and Simon with the Fuchs family. Simon and Herman apprenticed in their tailor shops. To be an apprentice at an early age as they were, was not easy and not uncommon. In addition to needlework, and sewing they did in the shop, they were treated as servants yet each one became a highly skilled tailor able to make a man's suit to measure. Besides being highly skilled in their craft, they were and are good human beings.

Simon was self-reliant and unafraid. During those days a rare quality. I learned much from him; we all did. It was hard to match his optimism. Even under the worst conditions he never despaired, and if he did, no one was aware of it. He used to say certain things, such as "self pity will kill you" He was very protective of Herman, his younger brother. He never allowed him out of his sight. I think of them often, we are still friends.

In late December, Herman was transferred to the tailor shop. Simon was relieved; working in the tailor shop, Herman was spared from working in the mines and the horrible marches to and from.

The leader of Block #1 was Harry Mundt. Before the war, Harry was a stage actor in Budapest, his younger brother Shimi was a member of my hometown's soccer team.

I knew Shimi well, he used to call on one of the Shwartzberger sisters; they were our neighbors. On one of his visits he came with his brother Harry. The two brothers both blond looked very much alike. As leader of Block # 1, Harry was also instrumental in organizing a music and entertainment group. It was not so difficult to gather very talented individuals for the orchestra. The Nazis provided the musical instruments and those chosen to entertain the Nazi officers gladly participated.

The performers received no special treatment for their efforts, but had they been singled out for some benefits it would have been well deserved. On Sundays (not every Sunday) the sounds from the concerts filled the camp with hope. For a while I could forget where I was, but the feeling good period did not last long. After a concert, the drabness of our existence was ever present. The crematorium had been completed by then and in full use, and we became accustomed to the misery and dying. Harry knew all the Kapos and socialized with them. Eventually he behaved like a Kapo himself and began to mistreat inmates. In contrast Rado, a Jew also from Hungary, a tall mild mannered man, an exceptionally nice person, was the camp secretary (registrar). His function was to record and report to the military camp commandant.

In late January there were openings in the shoe repair shop; they needed additional help. After each work shift mounds of wood bottom shoes needed repair; while the inmates were sleeping their shoes were repaired and returned to the blocks and barracks they came from.

On a Friday night after roll call, Simon submitted my number for a possible transfer to the shoe repair shop. I knew if Rado were to submit my camp ID number I would have a better chance.

Since I didn't know Rado personally I decided to talk to Harry Mundt first, and hoped that he would remember me. It was an opportunity I did not want to miss. I ran across the appel platz to Block #1. Because of his position, Harry had a small private room. I was scared to knock on his door. What if he's in a bad mood, how will he react to my request? I knocked on the door and entered. He looked at me with indifference. I told him who I was, I gave him my full name, when I mentioned his brother by name and told him that I remembered his coming to Besztercze to visit his brother Shimi the soccer player, I noticed a change in his expression; He asked what I wanted. I told him that the shoe repair shop was taking on more people and would he help me get transferred. I asked him to talk to Rado and tell him that I'm in Block #5 and please give him my inmate number 75128. He said he would do what he could.

I thanked him, went back to my Block and hoped for the best. In less than an hour Rado stood by the entrance to my room with a piece of paper in his hand and called out my number 75128. He said he was looking for me and told me to go to the shoe repair shop before someone else took my place. I went to the shop, reported to the Kapo, and started to work on the night shift. In the morning I moved out of Block #5 to another barrack.

All the inmates who worked inside the camp: the kitchen personnel, the electricians, carpenters, tailors, shoemakers, infirmary attendants, those who disposed of the dead, were all called specialists.

We were housed in separate barracks, separated from the other inmates. Our food rations were the same, we had to stand for roll call as many times as the rest of the camp, but I was not exposed anymore to the daily, dangerous life threatening conditions of working underground in the tunnels. Working in the shoe repair shop was demanding. Large burlap bags, tagged with Block or Barrack numbers, were filled with shoes all needing repair. Since every shoe had a different problem, we had to be creative about how best to repair them. We had no machines of any kind; we had threads, awls, needles, tacks, and scraps of leather from discarded shoes. The volume that came to us every shift always overwhelmed us. Working hard, we managed to finish all the work. Had we left any work for the next shift, some of the shoes could have been misplaced. We did not want to have such complaints against us.

The Schuster Kapo, as everybody called him; that was his title. He was the most feared man in the lager (camp). To call him a sadist would be kind. He enjoyed inflicting pain and fear in everybody. He was a convicted German criminal, not a political prisoner. He probably was placed in the concentration camp for his talent of being unremorsefully cruel to others. He was short, used a cane and had a contorted walk. He took pleasure in beating up people, even the other Kapos feared him. If you were anywhere near him when he tripped or faltered walking, your life was in danger.

At night he used to roam the camp like a wildcat looking for its prey. Often he went to a barrack, dragged someone out of his bunk bed and beat him senseless with his cane. Everybody was at risk. Ironically he was protective of his workers, but we feared him anyway. When he was in the shop we did not dare speak among ourselves. In back of the shop, behind a glass door covered with a curtain, was the Kapo's private room. During the entire time I was in the shop I never saw anyone go inside that room other than Victor, the 14 or 15 year-old blond Ukrainian boy, who served the Kapo exclusively. He also entertained the Kapo by plucking a balalaika singing Ukrainian songs. From behind the door we used to hear the Kapo say, "spiel Victor, spiel" (play Victor play)

I had a lucky break. My transfer to the shoe repair shop came at a very critical time. I was on the brink of giving up, my physical deterioration had been gradual. I had been depressed, cold and hungry all the time. I neglected myself, I had not washed as I should have. Observing others I could see the remarkable changes that took place in all of us. Unless we were forced to run, everyone walked slower. I could see a gradual deterioration in others, but not in myself. I was not aware of my condition until Simon, with his straight forward comment, said to me "Shimi, you better watch out, you look like a Muselmann" a term used to describe the walking dead.

The weeks I worked in the shop gave me a chance to recuperate. After a day's or night's work, depending on the shift, I returned to my warm barrack. A red hot potbellied wood burning stove was In the middle of the barrack radiating warmth throughout. The barrack was clean, the bunk beds comfortable. Everybody called the barrack caretaker Stary. In Slavic I think it means old fellow. Stary was very jealous of his domain. While long icicles hung from the roof shingles outside, and the windows were all steamed up, he was the person who kept the fire going and the barrack spotlessly clean and warm.

82

The barrack was like an oasis in hell. Soon as I stepped outside, I was painfully aware of the contrast. I could have been also there outside with all the others, the endless degradation all around, everywhere. Fellow inmates just returning from working in the tunnels, shivering and dirty, scurrying to get out of the cold, only to repeat and be part of the same misery tomorrow, and endless tomorrows. As for myself working in the shop was much safer, but I was very insecure, I feared that at any moment some unforeseen punishment could banish me back into the tunnels.

Chapter 5

FROM MELK TO NOWHERE

Many of the civilian engineers, supervisors, came from the Alsace Lorraine region, sometimes they shared the news of the war with us. Since they were away from home for long periods of time they were also eager for the war to end. I didn't realize it then, that those of us who could understand and speak German had an advantage, compared to those who didn't know the language. Knowing the language, hearing a command in German, even the body language of a commanding officer had meaning,

On the Soviet front the German armies suffered one defeat after another. The Russians were pushing relentlessly towards Vienna, and on the Western front the British and American forces were also advancing. All that information came from the civilian Foremen from (schachtbau)

The news was very encouraging. It gave us hope that the war would not last much longer and the Nazis would be defeated. Now all we had to do was to be careful, not get into trouble, and survive one day at a time. I began to wonder how it would be to go home be reunited with my family and be free again.

The German Armies were in retreat; On April 13, 1945 the Red Army liberated Vienna. The Melk sub camp was not far from Vienna. In a matter of days at most, we hoped to be freed. If my father and I were lucky to live through this nightmare, I was sure we'd find each other soon. I had to be hopeful, hope was good nourishment.

Days before the area around Melk was overrun by the Soviets, the Germans evacuated our camp. On a Friday, the first week in April 1945, in the first of two groups, we marched down to the banks of the Danube River. Four cargo river barges, their decks loaded with lumber were waiting for us. We had no idea where we were going and why on boats. Going upstream on the Danube meant only one thing, they were taking us further, deeper into Austria.

In great haste they gave us a piece of sausage and bread. Before we went down on a narrow ladder I wolfed my ration. In semi darkness we settled in. Hours later, buckets of water with tin cups were passed down to us. Since we were not allowed on deck, I tried to sleep most of the time down there. The roar of the engines and the stench from human waste became unbearable. Once a day we were allowed on deck for 15 minutes; three days later we arrived in Linz. As we climbed out of the barges we were handed a ration of bread, a small piece of wurst and a piece of margarine. I was surprised that we even got that much to eat, for three days we had nothing except water and that also was rationed by the cupful. Then I remembered Simon's advice not to save any bread for later, he used to say, "What is in your stomach counts not what is in your pocket" I ate every morsel.

Very quickly we were lined up in rows of five and began our march. Although weakened by days in the hold of the barge the first afternoon was not bad. I felt invigorated by the fresh spring air, the road was level and we had nothing to carry except ourselves. The ever present guards on both sides of the column were also on foot, with heavy backpacks and rifles. The Austrian countryside was beautiful, the roads well paved, the fields beginning to green, and the farm houses were all well kept. We still did not know where our final destination would be.

On the road, there was hardly any civilian traffic. Military vehicles went in both directions; loaded trucks with battered soldiers coming from the front did not look so mighty any more. At times there was so much traffic we had to stay on the side of the road until the traffic cleared. That part of Austria, the rural areas with its mountains and lakes, had not been touched by war.

Everybody appeared to be all right so far. We were not rushed; the changing scenery, the perfect fields, and the farmhouses like painted landscapes. The sun was warm; other than being very hungry, I felt good. We marched all afternoon till evening; by then we were off the main road marching on narrow country roads with farms all around us.

For the first night they put us up on a large farm. We were given something to eat, I can't remember what, then we gathered around an outdoor fountain with troughs full of water. We washed the grime off ourselves and we settled in for the night. I was sure the family inside the big farmhouse saw us. Behind the curtains the lights were on, they might have been told not to come out. I had no idea how many we were in that transport. We occupied outside buildings, an empty equipment shed, a hayloft, and another outdoor building. I spent the night in the large hay loft, the smell of hay reminded me of home. Hay has a special scent like dried herbs. I was tired from the long three day boat ride and the march this far. We were crowded, but I had the best night's sleep in a week.

In the morning, we began to come out one by one from barns, tool sheds, and haylofts; reluctantly we lined up in rows of five and began to march. The morning air was refreshing, we marched until noon without stopping. On the open road the sun turned from pleasantly warm to torturously hot. Marching five in a row with locked arms was as bad as being chained to one another, yet holding on that way we also supported each other. We still had no idea where they were taking us; if one asked they wouldn't tell us.

Walking with eyes closed, a minute or two of sleep here and there, was good. We stopped only when the guards were tired and wanted to rest. Then for no reason they began to speed up the march. When we could barely walk, they forced us to march faster and faster. If they knew that their days were numbered why did they do this? This forced hike turned into a death march. Stupefied from exhaustion, men began to drop to the ground, others unable to go further staggered to the side of the road and risked being shot by the guards. Occasionally we would hear rifle shots, we prayed the shots were not for those who could no longer walk.

I was very frightened, my legs moved me along without me knowing it. We had one stop by the side of the road, and after about ten minutes, when it came time to stand up, my legs were cramped, I could hardly stand. The march became more painful by the minute.

There was absolutely nothing we could do, again we tried to slow down but the guards pushed us on.

We marched past farms and farm houses; not once did I see civilians (Austrians) in the fields or anywhere. Back in my home town, before we were deported when Russian prisoners of war were marched through the city, my townspeople tried to help the prisoners by throwing food to them. The Austrians were not of the same character. They had to know that we were starving; I believe they hid themselves from us. At the end of the second day, again we were herded into farm sheds and hay lofts for the night. The last day before we arrived in Ebensee, we dragged ourselves through a winding steep mountain road. We could no longer hold on to each other, we could not help each other as we had done before.

The day we were ordered to evacuate from Melk I was separated from my friends and those who knew me. I was alone, there was nobody in this group that I had known before. No one knows how deep one can reach to find the strength and will to keep going. Those who had fallen, the guards shoved out of the way, into the ditch. I often wonder what happened to those we left behind.

Chapter 6

EBENSEE

In the afternoon of the third day after we left Linz, we arrived in Ebensee. The camp was situated in the upper Austrian Salzkamergut Mountains, a few Km. Uphill from the town of Ebensee. Just like the other camps, this one also was surrounded by an electrified chain-link fence, and with guard towers on the other side of the fence. I also noticed that the guard posts were closer to each other than in Melk. The barracks were long wooden structures, scattered among tall pine trees. The toilets and washrooms were located between the barracks. Inside the barrack, wooden bunk beds placed very close together, one could hardly stand between them. We were crammed four to a mattress, two heads at each end. The mattresses were filthy. My barrack was somewhere in the middle of the camp. Two days after I arrived the second transport arrived from Melk, then the third. My friend Simon's transport came by train.

All the inmates worked in the tunnels. When the new transports came from Mauthausen and other sub camps, the camp population expanded to a point where less work sites were available. If you were lucky to have been selected for work, any kind of work, you could have received a plate of lukewarm water with a few potato peels floating in it. Starvation was now more real than in the previous camps I had been in. There was nothing at all to eat and many became so weak they could not get out of their bunk beds in the morning. Those who could, helped remove all who died during the night. In spite of the large increase in the numbers dying every day, many were still laying on the bare floor, the barracks were still over populated because of the many thousands who had been evacuated from other sub camps to Ebensee.

I was desperate, I had to put something into my stomach, I had to do something other than wait to die. For a chance of being assigned to a work detail I used to get up early and stand in front of the main gate and hope I'd be selected. Once outside the camp there was a chance I could find something, anything I could chew on and digest. Many chewed on pieces of coal found along rail tracks, and even green grass some plucked off the field like cattle in a pasture.

One day I was taken to a nearby rail line that was damaged by allied bombing; another day I was taken to fill bomb craters in the road. We never completed or repaired anything. We were many in number, but we had no strength to do any meaningful work. I could not hold a shovel in my hands, let alone use it. If we had to lift or move something, what three or four could have accomplished before, ten of us could not do now. When I found pieces of coal I chewed on them. I looked for and found garbage dumps with old chicken bones, vegetable waste, potato peels; it was much better than nothing. My friend Joe Kupfersmith barely survived by eating tiny snails he found on the backs of leaves of grass. Those finds were rare treasures. That way we could survive another day and another day closer to freedom.

Then, for two days in a row, I was not selected for work. Standing by the gate early in the morning made no difference anymore, very few went out to work. Upon my return to the barrack I found that one of the other three men that shared my mattress had died during the night. His body was now lying outside with the other dead. Every barrack had their dead laid out. They were mere skeletons with no weight to them. We had to take them to the crematorium, which was at a distance. I clearly remember how at first we tried to lift the corpses off the ground. Four of us couldn't lift a skeletal corpse, instead we dragged them on the ground between the pine trees to the crematorium. Corpses were already stacked like cordwood there. The shock and horror of that sight is still vivid in my memory. The crematorium was burning body's non-stop.

The dead were piled up so high we could not lift them onto the pile, we just left them there on the ground near the crematorium. We dragged the dead skeletons through the forest all day long.

There I was among the many thousands of starving people, some without any clothes, aimlessly staggering among the pine trees. What have they done to us, to reduce us, to exist at that level? To feel a loss of life is a human quality. With each corpse that I helped drag to the crematorium, I became more hardened and emotionally numb. As a survivor I paid dearly; a good part of my sensitivity and compassion is still in that dreaded forest of the death camp at Ebensee.

The following morning I lined up again in front of the gate hoping that I might be selected to work outside the camp. Others had the same idea and we all lined up automatically five in a row. Only outside the camp was it possible to find something to eat: a garbage heap with some old bones I could chew on.

I knew that bones any kind, were a good source of calcium. While we were waiting at the gate, someone from a couple of rows in back called out my name: "Mayer" I turned around wondering who could be calling my name. Those who knew me called me Shimi, nobody called me by my last name. Besides it had been days since I had seen anyone I knew from Melk. A person two rows behind me said, "Not you, I want the guy in front of you." I tapped the man's shoulder in front of me and said, "He wants you", pointing to the man in back. The person turned around, looking at me said, "I know you, aren't you Jacob's son?" Before I could say anything more he said, "Your father and I are cousins, my name is Martin". We spoke to each other in Hungarian.

I was surprised and speechless. He told me to stay close to him, and soon, after we leave the camp we'll have a chance to talk. He was right, we did go out together to a work site that day. That group was in the process of building a large wooden structure with stairs from one ground level to another.

The project made no sense at all. We knew it, the civilian supervisor knew it also, but it gave us a chance to leave the camp and be away from the dead and dying for a day. The second tier of steps was nearly finished. We were on a level about 15 meters above ground. Once we reached the top we sat down and did nothing. A Kapo or a German officer coming toward us or even just passing by, would have been spotted in advance. The steps we built were the only way to reach us.

The civilian supervisor didn't care if we worked or not. The sun was warm and the location looked like a perfect spot for a picnic, but with our empty stomachs that could only have been in a dream. Because we were assigned to the project, on our way out we did get a bowl of warm water with some potato peels floating in it. At the work site the foreman allowed us to look for whatever we could find to eat. Inside an abandoned tool shed we found a mound still somewhat frozen, with discarded scraps of vegetables and bones of unknown origin. It was good and we feasted on the find; it was a lot better than nothing. The Forman gave us a box of wooden matches, we made a small fire on the ground. We burned the bones to charcoal that way it was possible to chew on them.

The way I met Martin my father's cousin was extraordinary. I have never been so lonely and forsaken except when my father and I said goodbye to each other the year before in Melk. He appeared like an angel in human form. He was still in good physical condition. Martin was at least ten years younger than my father. I knew of him but did not remember having met him before. He and his family lived in Dej, a town halfway between Bistrita and Cluj. He was also evacuated to Ebensee from another Mauthausen sub camp. I stayed with his group for a few days—as long as was possible. He had appeared at a very critical moment; those few days positively extended my survival. He looked after me as well as he could.

A few days before we were liberated I saw my boyhood friend and schoolmate Eddy Goldstein. He was totally naked, leaning against a Pine tree. He barely could hold himself up. I saw others walking around naked, but when I saw Eddy without any clothes, that was different. He was my schoolmate and close friend. I spent many summer afternoons with him, rowing his canoe on the canal that bordered his fathers lumber yard. The last time I saw Eddy was about six weeks before, in Melk. He wasn't in very good shape then, but who was? He probably came over with the second or third transport. Now he was a skeleton, more than the human skeleton we had in anatomy class in high school. His ears were always big, we used to kid him about that, now they appeared much larger. His eyes were deep in their sockets as if trying to hide from the horror that enveloped us. Like a flimsy garment would cover one's nudity, so did the lifeless transparent skin, cover his skeletal body, and so desperate to find a place to rest. I tried to comfort him as he tried to speak. I heard him faintly but could not understand what he was saying. His voice was hardly a whisper; he was dying. I could not hold back my tears, we both cried. Looking at him I saw myself. One no longer measured survival by weeks or days: hours were the measure of how long one could last under those conditions. Despair and hopelessness was all around us; the walking dead, most without clothes in bare feet and in search of a scrap of anything, just something to eat. There were rumors of cannibalism, some of the corpses had missing buttocks. Personally I never witnessed this, but it was entirely possible.

The time came when nobody left the camp to work on any kind of project. We could feel the tension, the German officers did not enter the camp any more, they just stayed on the other side of the gate.

Our camp leader was a Frenchman from Strasbourg, also a prisoner, an imposing figure. Everybody seemed to like him. He always wore a dark blue French beret.

On that particular morning the SS camp commander ordered the entire inmate population to assemble on the appel-platz. We stood there for many hours. Usually the SS officers entered the camp and gave their orders and other business of the day. On that day the SS did not show, we just stood there waiting. All who could gather enough strength dragged themselves or were helped by others to the appel platz. Then Camille, sometimes we also called him the Frenchman, ordered us to return to our barracks. Word was passed around that no matter what happened, even if the guards were to use force to get us out of the barracks, we should refuse and stay put. We were to resist any attempt by the Germans to lead us out of the camp.

We stayed inside the barracks for the rest of the day and into the night. The silence was deadly. The situation was tense. Of the thousands of inmates not one dared leave his barrack. Fear and hope were equally strong. All other nights the floodlights were on, that night they were off. The camp was in complete darkness. We had the feeling that something was about to happen, but what? I was fearful and very anxious. I did not sleep that night and I know that there were many others who did not sleep also. At the first light of day a huge wavelike roar was heard coming from every direction. There was absolute chaos, people were screaming on top of their voices: "The guards are gone, we're free" I could not understand how the Nazis would just leave us there. With some caution we exalted, we cried, we embraced each other. We began to realize that the moment we waited for so long has finally arrived. All our suffering, humiliation and degradation had come to an end.

I left my barrack and walked through the camp in search of Martin Mayer my father's cousin, and my friends Simon and Herman. People roamed about like crazy, everybody was curious to know what really happened. We did not trust ourselves, we were afraid the guards would come back. As the hours passed, we assured ourselves that it was all over and we were free.

I wandered through areas of the camp I had not dared go to before. I came upon a former small food storage house, which had already been stormed by others. People were lying on the ground, trampled by the hungry mob. Shelves which had some loafs of bread before were empty by the time I got there, except for a few jars with skull and cross bone labels marked Gift (poison) on them, probably was rat poison. Fortunately

I could read the labels. In anger I smashed the jars against the wall. In another section there were a few sacks of flour on the floor in a corner. We wanted to take some flour back to the barrack with us but we knew we could not carry much weight. We shared the flour. Some poured it into their caps; what was left in the sack we dragged back to the barrack. We mixed the flour with water, and from the paste we made little flat breads in our metal soup plates. We ate them before they were baked; we could not wait, we were starving.

While some of us rejoiced, enjoying the first moments of freedom others sat around lethargically, picking lice from their thorn filthy shirts, not knowing what to make of the feeling—this feeling of fear that haunted all of us.

Chapter 7

LIBERATION

The traumatic events of the day before, became clear to us. Ganz the SS camp commander had ominous plans for us. Large amounts of dynamite had been planted at the entrance to a tunnel where they had planned to walk us inside and blow up the entrance. Another diabolic scheme this time they did not succeed.

On May 5, Ganz told Camille, our camp secretary that we should all go into the tunnel: since the shooting war (with the Americans) was getting closer; we'd be safer underground. By then Camille was aware of the Nazi plot, which was why the day before he had dismissed us from roll call without the Nazi commander's permission. During the night most of the guards and Nazi officers escaped into the woods. American units caught many of them wearing civilian coats over their SS uniforms. Later my friend Simon told me that he was assigned to a work unit, and did not know for what purpose they had placed crates with explosives (dynamite) at a tunnel entrance.

On May 6, at about noon, I heard a loud crashing sound that came from the main gate. I was curious I went in that direction. It was like a recurring nightmare, I thought the Germans had returned. I saw a tank that had just crashed through the gate, rumbling toward the open space of the appel-platz making a half turn facing in our direction and stop. From where I stood I could not tell whether it was a German or an American tank. Then I saw the hatch open and two soldiers came out and looked around. From everywhere people made their way toward the tank. I was stunned; I realized the army tank with a large white star on its side had to be American. Everybody was yelling "the Americans are here" Like a mob they surrounded the tank, some attempted to climb on top of it. The two soldiers quickly climbed back inside and closed the hatch.

Barrack #1 faced the appel platz and it was the first barrack near the gate. I was standing nearby, a good spot from where I could see how the tank maneuvered its way around the appel platz. To get a better view a number of guys made their way to the roof of the barrack. They were screaming, all excited, thrusting their arms in the air, yelling incoherently, when I saw this one fellow loose his balance, collapse onto the roof, roll down and fall to the ground dead; I couldn't catch my breath. Others rushed to his side, we saw he needed help but it was too late, he didn't move he was dead.

For months I had witnessed brutal beatings, tortures; I had seen people die in horrific ways. And now, after all that man's suffering, what a cruel joke to see him die that way. He survived the camps but could not live to be free.

During that afternoon more tanks came up the mountain road to the camp. That very afternoon the desire for revenge was boiling over. The Kapos who were so cruel were hiding or trying to escape, some of them did succeed but others were captured. The schuster kapo from Melk whom I had not seen since we left Melk was clubbed to death. It was a gruesome sight, I did not witness the beating, but I saw his body on the ground after they were finished with him. It was the bloodiest mess I ever saw. He deserved to die; back in Melk he killed innocent people just for sport.

Next day, the American army set up field kitchens. The aroma of good food permeated the air. No one realized, including our liberators, that the food was too rich for our stomachs of starving people. We were fed well and too often. We did not use the metal camp plates, we ate from shiny aluminum plates the Americans gave us. All day and into the night we were given hot meals, meat and potatoes, cooked vegetables, all that anyone wanted to eat. After that first feast many did not show up again for meals, because many became very sick. Then the Army Red Cross urgently set up first aid stations and hospitals. Under long tents, hundreds of field cots were quickly occupied.

A few times I went inside those hospital tents; hoping I may find someone I knew. When I saw the many sick laying on those cots, I realized how fortunate I was to be able to walk on my own and not needing hospital care.

The American soldiers were most kind and generous. The day they liberated us, they touched our hearts. We cried, they cried with us. They carried our sick in their arms: they washed them, cared for them and were most gentle with them. They gave us life and restored hope. I will always be grateful for that. I wonder how many young Americans know what their fathers and grandfathers accomplished during World War II in Europe. The American army had just defeated the most vicious and barbaric German power, and within hours the Americans showed their humanity. As long as I live I will remember that day. Had the American army taken one or more days to reach us, hundreds, perhaps thousands more, including myself, would have died.

I think it most appropriate to mention Dr. William V. McDermott of Dedham, Massachusetts a true American hero. During the war he was a surgeon in the US Army. In his book; 'A Surgeon in Combat' published in 1997, vividly describes his medical unit, among the first to arrive and help the survivors of the concentration camp in Ebensee.

After so many years reading the chapter about Ebensee, describing the misery and horror he found there, jarred my memory, I was taken back to that hell. After reading his book I had the honor to communicate and thank him for his kindness and selfless contribution in helping the survivors of Ebensee.

The cremation of corpses was halted. Austrians, including the Mayor of Ebensee were forced to come to the camp and dig graves for those who had to be buried. They were made to come and see for themselves the horrible atrocities their citizens committed.

On the fourth or fifth day after we were liberated, I ventured to walk out of the camp with a few other guys just to see what the outside world looked like. Going downhill on the main road we could manage, we stopped a few times. For the first time in over a year we walked without armed guards at our side, a new feeling that didn't take long to get used to. We couldn't go far. We had to rest often, we decided it would be best if we returned to the camp. Now that the camp food was so delicious we didn't want to miss a meal. Going back uphill we had to rest often. On the left side of the road there were small wooden barracks, all alike and unoccupied. We later found out those civilian workers, engineers who worked in the tunnels were housed there. We entered one; it was furnished with bunk beds, clean blankets, a table and chairs, and a stove but with no personal belongings. We assumed nobody lived there. The beds were comfortable and we rested for a while. It was very inviting, It became too late in the day to go back to the camp so we decided to spend the night there. We had nothing to eat except a few chocolate bars and one fellow had a small can of instant coffee that the Americans had given us. We crossed the fields to a farmhouse and as soon the farmer saw us coming, he and his wife came out to meet us. We told them that we didn't come to cause any trouble, all we wanted was some food; we asked for bread, butter, eggs, milk, and nothing more. In a few minutes the farmer's wife brought out a basketful of stuff, they were more than willing to give us that. We went back to our comfortable place and prepared our dinner. The small barrack was well stocked with dishes, utensils, pans and a coffee pot. We had scrambled eggs with bread and butter. After we had our dinner we boiled a pot of water and emptied the can of instant coffee into the pot. We enjoyed our meal, it was so good to be away from the camp. We talked all night until morning. Later I realized that due to the strong instant coffee we were awake all night. We liked our new accommodations and were reluctant to go back to the camp. We stayed another few days. We were puzzled about the fact that the farmer and his wife were so generous, without a hint of resistance they gave us what we asked for.

A few days later we found out that a group of Ukrainians also from the camp slaughtered a cow in a pasture and carried off the beef.

Before returning to camp we went to Gmunden, an old city with picture perfect Tyrolean houses. The streets were crowded with people of all ages, young and older men alike wore Lederhosen (leather shorts made of deer skin). The war had ended just about over a week or so ago, but they did not look like defeated people. There were no signs of war at all; compared to other towns that were bombed and had visible signs of destruction, Gmunden was untouched by war.

We then took a boat ride on the nearby Traunsee, a magnificent lake trapped between Tyrolean Mountains. The water bus made frequent stops along the coast line. It was a perfect day, the sun was bright, the air cool with not a cloud in the sky, one could not imagine a more peaceful place.

On the open deck people were sitting on long benches admiring the view. On a bench with his back to the water sat a man who looked familiar. I thought I knew this person but from where; then it came to me. There was no mistake about it; he was Herr Wolman, the leather merchant from my hometown. My father frequently bought leather and other supplies from his store. Although he was active in local Nazi activities, at first he dealt fairly with my father, nevertheless my father did not like to shop in his store. Our town had two leather supply stores, for some items my father had no choice but had to go to his store. Herr Wolman's son was among the first to volunteer to serve in the German army. In the last year before we were deported, Herr Wolman's behavior toward my father was not cordial.

In the fall of 1944 the Soviet army liberated my hometown. Wolman, and many others like him, Nazi sympathizers and collaborators, in fear of what the Russians might do to them, escaped westward. Many settled in Austria and Bavaria as refugees.

The more I remembered the angrier I became. As my rage increased by the moment, I was tempted to confront him. Thinking fast, how should I approach him? Should I say . . . Herr Wolman do you remember me? Of course you do . . . the many times I shopped in your store in Bistritz. Why did you treat my father with such disrespect? He was a loyal customer, he never owed you any money, Why did you insult my father; not with words but with indifference. He did not deserve that from you. Had my friends known what I was thinking they would have dealt with it differently; but this was my private war, I did not trust myself what I might do. I decided to leave him alone. I knew I was going home, but he never will. For the moment I was confused but pleased that I could control my anger. At the next stop we got off the boat.

The problem with factual testimony is this, how am I to describe the events with a language that is limited by my vocabulary? How can I describe what happened there and was still ongoing? I want to impress the reader to imagine the unimaginable. I try to describe using words like; pain, hunger, uncontrollable fear, cruelty and death. When total exhaustion invited "Death" into the barracks, "The death rattle" required too much energy; my bunk mates died one after the other without a murmur. There were moments I envied the dead; they suffered no more.

The Austrians in that area behaved as if nothing had happened, totally oblivious of the fact that in the mountains, a few kilometers away, there was a concentration camp where innocent people were still dying due to the atrocities their countrymen had committed. When we talked to the Austrians, their answer was always the same "wir haben nicht gewust"

(we didn't know). When did it become so easy for a people to lie? It was impossible for them not to have known; the camp was practically in their backyard. They had to know what happened in the camp, (in their back yard) I hated to be among them. I longed to return home soon as possible.

The few weeks after liberation were difficult. We all wanted to return to our homes and get on with our hopes and dreams. At the same time we deeply feared what and whom we would find or not find back home. Many labor camps throughout Austria and Germany that were liberated by the British, American and Soviet forces, with few exceptions were all death camps.

The Americans provided us with some clothes, nothing special. We had thrown our filthy lice infested striped camp clothes into a huge outdoor fire and watched them burn. I kept my shoes, I could not part with the shoes that had protected my feet throughout all . . . from Auschwitz to Mauthausen, Melk and Ebensee. When I think of the many ways I succeeded in holding on to my shoes! A few times my shoes were almost taken away from me, literally taken off my feet but I fought to save them. I truly believe having had my good shoes on, helped me come through winter months with snow, rain and mud. I shudder thinking of what might have happened to me had I had to struggle in those wood bottom clogs that barely stayed on. They were impossible to walk in. There were also others who managed to hold on to their own shoes. I thanked my lucky star every time I saw someone struggle walking in those miserable wood bottom shoes.

The dying and the very sick were treated with dignity. They received the very best care the American army doctors could provide. The threat of an outbreak of infectious diseases was real. The Americans encouraged those who felt well enough, to leave the camp and go home. I was ready to go home.

The Austrian transportation system had come to a halt; heavy allied bombing destroyed the main roads and rail lines. One of the inmates was a young Austrian from Bad-Ischel. He probably was a political prisoner. The day he was liberated he walked home, his town was only 17 Km. Away. I remember him saying: "How surprised my parents will be to see me" I wish I had learned more about this young man but I had only known him briefly.

As for myself I was weak, I had no physical pain except my legs had been ulcerated. That began months before in Melk. Scabs began to form but with time all healed without leaving any marks; except one that left a hole in my right leg. Eventually that one also healed, leaving a discolored scar on that spot.

Ebensee crematoria oven

Ebensee Survivors preparing a meal on an open fire (May 8,1945)

Ebensee Starved survivors (May 8,1945)

Ebensee Survivors in hospital barracks #2 (May 8,1945)

Ebensee Survivors outside a hospital tent (McDermott Collection)

Ebensee survivors, too weak to eat solid food, suck on sugar cubes (May 8,1945)

Ebensee survivors sorting clothes

Ebensee Roll Call Square—Day after Liberation

Chapter 8

GOING HOME

The Americans treated us well; they also encouraged us to make plans to leave. We were much too crowded, we were still three to four to each bunk bed. Sanitary conditions inside the bunks were not good, although we were preparing to go home we still wanted to stay a little longer. Most of us came from East-European countries. We had no illusions about what we may or may not find back home. Each day more truckloads left the camp—I also joined a group that was headed for Vienna. We were provided with food for the trip. Army trucks took us to Linz; that was as far as the Americans could take us. We did not know that from Linz eastward, Austria was occupied by the Soviets. When the Americans dropped us off we were on our own.

I was disappointed, we had hoped we'd be taken all the way to Vienna, and without American protection I felt insecure. In Linz we asked about transportation means to Vienna but, there were none, passenger trains were not running. We were of many opinions how to continue, we broke up into groups, four of us decided to walk on the rail tracks. From my geography and history lessons in high school, I knew that Austria was a small country known for Mozart, Vienna Waltz and the Alpine's Yodeling but because of my experiences in the camp I still feared the Austrians. To avoid their country roads and villages, we followed the train tracks to Vienna, that way we were sure we would not get lost. Late in the afternoon we came upon a railroad junction, rail workers were inspecting and coupling cars that were loaded with coal. They did not know when that train was going to leave but they assured us it was headed for Vienna. We made ourselves comfortable on top of the coals and hoped the train would leave soon. We fell asleep, not aware when the train began to move. With frequent stops the train moved slowly then sometime during the night a pouring rain woke us.

At one of the stops we had to get off, we were rested but soaking wet.

Broken down boxcars everywhere. Fleeing the rain we helped each other climb into one of the empty wagons. The boxcars were similar to the ones in which the Germans took us away. To this day when I see a boxcar train, that memory comes to the surface, with all the horrors of that journey to Auschwitz. When we saw each other at early dawn, we broke up laughing; covered with coal soot, we looked like chimney sweepers. After a while the rain stopped and we left the boxcar.

To our surprise we found ourselves in the huge rail yard outside Vienna. Workers in the yard told us that all the tracks were damaged and from there we'd have to walk to Vienna. Again we tracked along the damaged rails. I did not mind at all the delays to our travel; on the contrary I felt a sense of satisfaction seeing the material destruction of Austria, a small price to pay for their brutality during the war.

We came upon a destroyed bridge. To cross over to the other side we had to climb over large chunks of concrete blocks that had fallen in the shallow river. Once on the other side, the roads and streets were passable. Bombed out buildings and huge mountains of rubble and bricks everywhere. Soviet forces occupied Vienna. It was the first time that I saw Russian soldiers in uniform. Large posters of Joseph Stalin were planted at street intersections and huge red flags draped public buildings from top to bottom. Civilian traffic was on foot or on bicycles. We walked through large sections with ruins of bombed out buildings, then some streets with buildings not damaged at all. It was still early in the morning; Soviet soldiers patrolled the streets on foot. Not they or anyone else bothered us. I drew my companion's attention to a soviet soldier sitting on a chair sleeping, with an automatic rifle between his legs, while guarding the entrance to that building.

We wanted to find the shortest way to the South rail station. We were told that from there trains were running to the Hungarian border and to Budapest.

We walked for hours, about noon we reached a secluded little park with benches and a water fountain. The day was warm and pleasant. We stripped to the waist and took turns at the water pump to wash off the accumulated dirt. A passing woman approached us saying she heard us speak Hungarian, she wanted to know where we were from. I told her in German that we were from Siebenburgen (Transylvania); she told us she also came from that region, her two sons had volunteered to serve Germany and both were killed on the Russian front. She herself was a refugee and lived in a one room apartment in a building just around the corner from the square. She invited us to go with her if we wanted a bowl of soup.

Apparently some residential areas were not bombed, four and five story old buildings all intact not a hair out of place. Her apartment seemed to be very small, we sat around a small kitchen table. While she prepared the soup she told us how in 1943 the Saxons were encouraged to send their young men and women to serve the 'Reich' (we knew that, my neighbors also volunteered to serve Nazi causes for the glory that was to last a thousand years) She was friendly, she cried and said she was homesick also. We had not had anything to eat since we left Linz, we were hungry and accepted her offer. She made us kimel (caraway seed) soup, that was all she had. The hot plate of soup was good, it was the only warm liquid we had since we left Ebensee. We thanked her and went our way.

If there were any organized aid stations for returnees like us, we did not know of them.

Finally we reached the station with trains full of refugees, we boarded one for Budapest. In Austria and crossing into Hungary again no one bothered us about tickets, on arriving to Budapest we were guided to a welcome station and communal kitchen. There we were fed well and spent the night in a large building that was set aside for returnees from German camps.

We were told that the American Joint Distribution Committee funded the operation. We were assigned beds and went to sleep. Evidently the old buildings in Budapest were infested with bedbugs. I never saw bedbugs before.

I don't know why they are called bedbugs, they were in the furniture, chairs, bed frames, inside the walls and under the wallpaper. In the dark of night they crawled out. To keep them from coming out, a single light bulb hanging from the ceiling was left on all night.

I had no desire to hang around the Hungarian capital. After breakfast a few of us went to the train station, and boarded a train to the Romanian border. We crossed into Transylvania and made our way to Cluj. At the border between Hungary and Romania again nobody asked us for personal identification or train tickets.

In September 1944, Transylvania had been liberated by the Soviets. Nine months later June 1945, for those who were not in concentration camps, daily life had long returned to near normal. Cluj was a lively bustling city. As a young boy I had been to Cluj once with my father. These were not ordinary calendar dates. Had my family been able to hide out somewhere, for those four months from May to September 1944, we could have escaped deportation to Auschwitz.

For four of us our ultimate destination was Bistrita, my home town. The last bus had already left and there was no train service until the next day. Sixty kilometers from my town, from home . . . I could not accept being so close and yet still so far. It was getting dark, the four of us were standing next to our belongings on the sidewalk of a busy street, and trying to figure out our next move. A delivery truck pulled up next to us. On its side a sign in bold letters read "Bere Bistrita"

Bere Bistrita was the name of the only brewery in town. Before we were deported the Brecher family owned the brewery, the beer was of high quality and very popular. In the fall of 1940, when our region was ceded to Hungary, the new school year had just begun when the official language changed from Romanian to Hungarian. My Hungarian vocabulary and grammar was less than acceptable, I needed private tutoring.

Eva, the daughter of Mr. Brecher owner of the brewery, offered to tutor me free of charge in her home. On one occasion Eva's father interrupted the lesson just to inquire how we were progressing. He asked if I would take a short dictation, I accepted the challenge. The dictation went well until mid sentence when he said, "vesszo" (comma). Instead of using the comma sign I wrote "vesszo" (comma spelled in full). I was very embarrassed but Eva and her father understood that the dictation made me a little nervous. How strange, I still remember what had happened five years earlier but how could I not remember . . . Her father was a prominent and admired person in the community and Eva their only daughter was a kind and beautiful young person.

In early spring of 1944 her father was among the first to be arrested by the local Fascist police; how sad not one of that family survived. Now the brewery was managed by a communist "cooperative" a business model I was to understand soon. Many privately owned business properties like the brewery, passed from private to collective ownership.

The driver had just finished making his beer delivery and was in the process of hoisting the empty wooden beer barrels onto the open truck. We tried to get his attention but he wouldn't listen and refused to take us. We then climbed on the truck and pleaded with him to drive us to Bistrita, claiming it was more important for us to get home than his empty beer barrels. After some arguing he agreed, we sat on top of the barrels and were on our way. This was the last leg of our voyage. By then it was dark, we passed through Gherla, Dej, Beclean, towns with familiar names, but nothing could distract me from my impatience and desire to get home.

It was past midnight when we arrived in Bistrita, everything appeared the same as it always had been, nothing appeared to have changed, or out of place. The air was fresh and clear I was back home. I tried to convince myself that the bad nightmare was over and nothing in this world could hurt me now.

The driver let me off next to the Lutheran church under the tower clock that was well lit in the center of town. I took my rucksack, jumped off the truck, thanked the driver, said goodbye to the other boys and started to walk toward my home.

At first I wanted to run, run home like I used to when I was late, but I enjoyed the walk. I glanced toward my father's shop next to Tzikely's bookstore; the metal shutters were rolled down as always, that time of night. I looked at every building around me. I looked at the cobblestones in the road I walked on. Ten or more years before, as a boy I spend hours watching men lay the stones in an arched pattern. First they dug up and hauled away the old surface, then the shaped stones were placed closely together in a layer of fine sand. Every time I walked or rode my bicycle on that surface I remembered the men who so diligently worked on that road. The shops were all closed. I imagined how lively the streets would be in a few hours. In a whole year nothing had changed. The walkway under the arches looked deserted as always that time of night.

At the all-night open drug store on the corner, I saw there was someone on duty, the night-light was on. If one needed something, filling a prescription or buying aspirin in powdered form, the only way it was available then. Darmol was the most popular laxative (on it's package the printed message read 'while you sleep Darmol works') all you had to do was knock on the wooden doors and the Apotheker (druggist) would take care of you. The muffled sounds of the night and the smells were so familiar, for a moment it was so easy to forget that I had been away, and just returned from hell.

Past the corner drugstore I turned right, into the street without a name. On that short street there were no house numbers. The street had a narrow concrete sidewalk on one side only. Once riding my bicycle, to avoid hitting a pedestrian, I scraped my knuckles raw against that brick wall. The street was too rough to ride on. At the end of this narrow street is Strada Elizabeta, (Erzsebet Utca in Hungarian) at this intersection was this nice stucco house with garden all around, and enclosed with a wrought iron fence.

The corner street light made the black fence shine as if freshly painted; all was so familiar and peaceful. Now I was on my street and two more short blocks ahead, house number 35 was my home.

My rucksack was light on my back, it was almost empty except for a shirt and a dirty towel. My chest was pounding harder the closer I came to my home. I passed the low shuttered windows, the framed French styled glass windows opened to the inside. That time of the year we kept them open, and the shutters were also left open enough to let the cool evening air through. Past the tall wooden fence that covered the yard from view was the gate door that just wouldn't open. It was never easy to push open. At my first try I was not surprised, but after repeated shoves and pushes the gate door still would not budge. It was stuck, and after more forceful pushing I managed to get it open wide enough to squeeze through. I pushed my way through the tall weeds, past the old apple tree in the middle of the yard, past the open verandah (porch) then onto the cement walk toward the kitchen door. The same door through which we were taken away the year before.

Our house was an old house with stucco walls and a weathered wood shingled roof. The kitchen was the most important room for us and was quite large. We had all our meals in the kitchen, we had no formal dinning room. On Friday nights and holidays my mother lit and blessed the Sabbath candles and after we returned from the synagogue we had our holiday meal. Throughout the week we seldom had our meals together.

As children we could do different things there and not be in the way. My mother did her cooking and baking, and we could do our homework, school projects and still not be in her way. In winter the kitchen was the most comfortable room. We also had a large wood burning terra cotta oven located in an open corner from were all three bedrooms could be heated warmly.

The large kitchen door was not locked, I pushed it wide open, I reached for the light switch and nothing happened. A heavy musty damp smell permeated the room. I called out "anyone home" I called out several more times the silence was alarming. I had hoped and wished for this moment for so long; to be welcomed home. (The reader may wonder why I had not telephoned home to announce my arrival: We had no telephone and most of the private homes in town had none) I had never been away from home for more than a week or two before deportation, and now . . . my enthusiasm turned into despair and terrible loneliness. I felt no hunger no thirst, but completely exhausted. In the dark I dropped to the floor near the open door, I placed the rucksack under my head and cried myself to sleep. At daybreak I went through the house, everything was in shambles, all the rooms were trashed, the heavy mahogany closets (two armoires) were broken into pieces, any furniture that couldn't be moved easily was destroyed; even the floor boards were ripped off the floor. The house was empty no sign of life, I longed to hear human voices, their coming and going the imagined sounds are filling all the empty spaces, how I wished that, that were true. Like a frightened child I called out their names one by one, the silence was more than I could bare, hours past, what will I do all alone? There was none to share my grief with. I was the youngest, my mother . . . how I used to cling to her. Oh, in the cattle car the last hours we spent together before arriving to Auschwitz; how she cried how abandoned and forsaken we all were. I am in my late seventies, as I write these lines I still feel the pain, the hurt that never goes away.

I explored my neighborhood, up and down the street, where a few Jewish families had lived, it was no different. The houses were broken into, vandalized, they were all empty of life. Apparently no one had returned. I started to knock on our non Jewish neighbors doors, I was surprised to see some abandoned their homes, no one to talk to. In the few hours since my return, from the outside everything appeared normal but the people who lived in the houses up and down the street, and the empty Jewish homes told a different story.

Our immediate neighbors the Hoch brothers; the Fritch families, the retired watchmaker and his wife, the chimney sweeper and his wife, were all Saxons; I soon realized that Saxons. (FolkDeutche) Nazi sympathizers who in fear of what the Soviets (Russians) might do to them, left with the retreating Germans; they were all gone. Hungarians, who openly supported the Hungarian Fascist government also were gone. Romanian families now occupied some of those houses. I walked the streets I wanted to see and talk to people, I wanted to share the news of my triumphant return, but nobody was interested.

I walked through the park, the "Alee" that I loved so much and spent many happy days with friends there. I sat on the bench where we usually met on weekends to play chess; I even thought about going up the Schiefferberg I was not ready for that; what would I be doing there alone? I remembered and grieved for my high school friends and others who had not returned.

In my group of close friends I was the only one who survived. Ohlbaum Jeno and Simon Tibi both died in Bergen-Belzen, Eddy Goldstein starved to death in Ebensee. The Stupp brothers the Bergfeld brothers Mendi and Buntzi, Lili who contracted polio as a child, a very pretty girl, the Kahan family, Chaim, Nuchem, Ossi and two other sisters; all the parents and grandparents of those I named and countless others whose names are blurred in my memory—none of them returned.

The war in Europe was over, Nazi Germany was defeated. To be a witness, to tell about Auschwitz, about the concentration camps, the horrible German atrocities, all seemed very important to me but I did not think I was up to the task. I was depressed. I missed everybody so much.

The city government was again under Romanian administration, and a Communist dictatorship; the neo-Fascists of yesterday became neo Communists. Positions in government were not earned through democratic elections but through membership in the all powerful Communist party. Many people did not like the system, but for the moment everybody appreciated the security the Soviet military occupation provided.

We met regularly at the Jewish community center in town, for a free meal, for lunch or supper. There the mood was different more hopeful. There were other survivors who before deportation lived in communities, villages outside the city. Some arrived just that morning, Good to be back one said, we exchanged stories and experiences; our tragic losses had changed us. We cursed the Nazis, then we felt good to be home and free.

My brother Bumi; after all he must be alive, he's just late in returning home. He was in a Hungarian military labor brigade, he was not deported to Auschwitz, and he must be somewhere. Many who were in the same situation had returned. Some had been back for several months. I had to find out more about him.

As for my father, last I heard from him was in Melk last December. It's very possible that he also will come home. My cousin Ibi was my age, perhaps she went home to Zalau, I should find out. I did not have much hope for my mother and my sister Rifku (she was so delicate and fragile) or my grandmother since no one of her age was spared; they were all gassed and cremated within hours after we arrived in Auschwitz. For my brother and father I was more hopeful, I was not ready to accept that I'll never see them again, it was too soon to give up hope.

When I left Ebensee there were hundreds who were too sick and too weak to leave. After liberation many survivors suffered serious psychological trauma and required months, in some cases years of treatment in mental institutions. I know of many who survived the camps and had to be hospitalized, some were taken to Sweden for treatment.

Mendi Gruber, we were once classmates in elementary school, I think I saved him from serious injury. When we were about ten years old, we played in the street, Mendi was too close to, and touched an exposed electric utility cable that hung from a street poll. After liberation he also was sent to Sweden but did not return home. I often wonder what happened to him? Every day a few more survivors returned, with a little luck some of my family could have survived. It may take months before I'd know for sure.

I spent much time around the house; it felt good to be home again but without my family it was just a place I used to call home.

To my surprise the hidden room behind the pantry closet was intact, the barrel of wine was safe on the ground just the way we left it. The sack of walnuts was chewed to bits by mice, only nutshells were on the floor. The plum preserves my mother made were in glass jars on the shelves, they were intact. The down filled comforters that we draped over wooden bars were completely shredded by moths or whatever, only shreds that looked like cobwebs were still hanging from the bars. Rodents consumed the sack of flour, onions and other edibles. The metal box under the floor boards in our bedroom with 60,000 Pengo Hungarian paper currency and 3,200 in American dollars was gone. My father was sure it was a good hiding place.

In 1945, the Romanian currency was again the Lei, and the currency in Hungary had been changed to the Forint. Had I found the box with the hidden cash, the dollars would have been a fortune, but the 60,000 Pengo, paper currency, my father's hard earned savings, a fortune a year earlier, now would have been worthless paper.

Then I began to look for the pot with my family's jewelry: my father's gold watch and chain, the broad sterling silver collar that adorned my father's talith (prayer shawl) and a few other items. I did not find it where I thought my father and I buried it. After each search in a different place, I was less sure where to look for it. I never found the earthen pot with the hidden treasure.

The lost objects had great sentimental value but as material value the objects became less important to me. My father owned a set of encyclopedia "Pallas Athena" which had been on a low shelf in the armoire. These books were also gone. They were leather bound with gold leaf lettering on the covers. We valued those books, for us they were an open window to the world. I was extremely careful when I leafed through the pages. I don't remember having had other books in the house. We had our text books for school my sister was reading novelettes, we listened to the radio, we had religious texts, we had no time for idle reading.

Opposite our home, across the street next to the red brick school building, was this large old house much nicer than the newer villas on the street. Preotul (Reverend) Flamand and his family lived there. That family was the liveliest on the street. Their son Mircea and their daughter Ileana had been at the university out of town, but when back home they lived carefree, often carelessly. Their mother used to confide to my mother how worried she had been about her son and daughter. Their behavior did not reflect well on their father's prestige in the community. The parents were relieved when they were away in school out of town.

The mother, the Preoteasa, ran the house with two servants and a full-time Gardner; the grounds were large compared to other houses in the neighborhood. The garden was separated by a low wooden fence that stretched all the way to the end of the schoolyard. The ground in front, between the house and fence facing the street, was cultivated with flower beds and rose bushes in many shades of color. Further back was the vegetable garden and fruit trees. In sunny spots they grew sunflower plants; the tall stalks with huge bright yellow flowers could be seen from the street. We also had fruit trees, but they had a walnut tree, past the vegetable garden, past the apple and pear trees, stood this towering grand old walnut tree. I knew when the walnuts would begin to fall to the ground, the preoteasa used to invite me to pick them up; some of the walnuts fell dry and clear from the outer shell.

To open the shells that did not release the nuts, I used to stamp on them with the heel of my shoe or hit them with a stone; that part was messy because the soft outer shells exude a kind of dirty brown oil. If it got on my clothes the stains were impossible to remove; it took days of washing to get the stains off my fingers but it was worth it. We used to play a game rolling walnuts on the ground, similar to pitching coins against a wall. I had no difficulty recognizing my walnuts, they were the largest in the bunch.

During the Petru Groza regime, one of the short-lived governments of Romania after King Carol's forced abdication, and the ouster of the Liberal Party, Reverend Flamand became the president of the school system. My father was stunned to learn that politically our good neighbor was a neo-Fascist. Although the political party he represented was anti-Semitic, as a neighbor he was always correct vis-à-vis my parents. Shortly after, in less than a year in 1940, all changed again. This time the Northern part of Transylvania (including Bistrita) was ceded to Hungary, for Romanians who held government positions the reversal of fortune was considerable.

Everything else also changed very dramatically. For us Jews in particular everything also changed. In a short few years' life became unbearable and eventually we were deported to Auschwitz.

Now back from the camps I was searching for some connection. I had to see my walnut tree. I always felt it belonged to me partly. The walnuts had not fallen yet, it was too early in the season. The villa was now empty, the gardens neglected and the Flamand family was gone without a trace. All this somehow didn't make sense. Since the end of the war the Romanians regained that part of Transylvania they had lost to Hungary.

I was curious, I wanted to know what happened to the Flamand family;

I remembered they owned a farm in one of the Borgos to the North. On a market day I asked around if anyone knew the whereabouts of the Flamand family.

Those from that region usually came to town to sell farm produce, grains, lumber for fire wood and at times livestock also. Several market days later I followed a hunch, I rode out on a bicycle in search of the Flamands.

Paddling my bike on this dusty road, I remembered the many Sunday afternoons I'd been on that road with my school friends on bicycles. Now that they were all gone, killed in Auschwitz or in other concentration camps, I painfully realized how much I missed them.

The trees that lined the road were heavy with fruit. In past outings we used to park our bikes in the ditch along the road, and picnic on fruit of choice. Now I was alone on a mission, I had to find out if the Preoteasa was still alive.

There are several Borgos, one after another, villages of the same name with different prefixes or add-ons. Finally I was directed to a house just off the main road. From a distance the house appeared larger then the others I had just passed. It was set back behind an overgrown hedge. I leaned my bike against its own rest and walked toward the open sun-drenched porch.

I hesitated for a moment thinking . . . What will I say, how should I introduce myself? Five years have passed since I last saw the Preoteasa; for a moment I regretted having come all this way. Then the screeching screen door opened, with the Preoteasa standing in the doorway. She looked at me and asked if I was lost, maybe she could help me.

I called out to her "Madam Preoteasa". Then I said I came from Bistrita, my name is Mayer Samuila, and my family lived across the street from you on the Regina Maria. She raised her hands upward as in prayer "Doamne, Doamne, Dumnezeu bun" (good God, good God) several times, "vine inauntru"(come inside) "ce mare bucurie" (what great joy) she cried in her happiness. She spoke nonstop, half the time I could not understand what she was saying. She was so happy to see me but when I told her about my family, my mother and father, my sister, brother, grandmother—she knew us all. She cried uncontrollably. I feared if someone were to enter and find her in that condition, what would they think. I tried to calm her as she told me how sad and lonely she was also.

In 1940 when Hungary took over half of Transylvania, her husband, Ileana and Mircea, (her son and daughter) left for Romania, to Bucharest.

She stayed behind in Bistrita for a while, then moved to their farm in Borgo—to protect her property there. When the outcome of the war was predictable, she hoped her family would return home, now for more then a year she had not heard from any of them, as if they had disappeared from the face of the earth. As for the Preot (her husband), since he was such a political opportunist, now again politically on the wrong side, she feared the Communist government in Bucharest might have arrested him.

"Vrei ceva de beut? tie foame" "ce mare ai crescut, la urma cind te-am vazut erai un copil mic",(something to drink, are you hungry? You are taller, the last time I saw you, and you were a little boy"

"The last time I saw you madam, I was picking up walnuts off the ground in your garden, that was five years ago, I was fourteen then"

She finally calmed down, and invited me to the kitchen table. From the pantry she brought out a jar of cherry preserves and said, "This is from last years crop, this year we had few cherries" They were large black cherries in sweet syrup. She sat next to me at the table and watched me enjoy the delicacy. We spent a couple of hours talking; I had to tell her all about my family. She showed genuine empathy. When I left she walked me to my bicycle. On my ride back to Bistrita I had a lot to think about. I was glad I had made the effort to find her, and then to learn that she was a caring person, in spite of her own losses.

Days passed I didn't know what to do, I was not alone in this situation there were others, many others with similar losses of family members but I still hoped that someone, my brother, my father at lease one would return; individually they both were physically stronger then me. I got up in the morning, I didn't know what to do, at first I was happy to have come home, but after a while in my loneliness I began to roam the streets all day long.

Searching through trash, piled against our neighbor's wall, I found bits of broken dishes, kitchen utensils, torn prayer books, ripped and stained family photographs, and bits of letters from America. With a little effort I managed to patch together my aunt's address:

Mrs. Rose Hirsch, 5302-15Th. Ave. Boro Park Brooklyn, New York. With my limited knowledge of Hungarian, I sent off a letter to America, and within a few weeks I had an answer. My aunt was so happy to hear from me, she urged me to write often and about everything. We corresponded frequently, and often my aunt enclosed a ten dollar bill. To my surprise not all incoming mail was censored. Soon I had enough money for clothes, for household items and other daily necessities. I no longer depended on others. I stayed in the house and made small improvements. In case someone returned, they would find the house in better condition than I had.

In the middle of our yard our very old apple tree had a crown of branches and a good growth of leaves but no apples. The tree trunk had a large gaping gash at about shoulder high. The split was tightly packed with mud. It seemed strange at first, it looked as if someone had pressed mud into the split but why? With a piece of a twig I loosened and scraped the mud from the gash. To my surprise a tightly rolled bundle of five and ten dollar bills fell to the ground. As I unrolled the bundle the paper money fell apart into rotted shreds. I was puzzled for a moment, but then I knew; it had to have been my grandmother's, who tried to hide the money, her daughter (my aunt) in America, had sent to her over a long period maybe years. My poor grandmother, she saved all that money—how desperate she must have been. She hid her old age security in the trunk of our old apple tree.

The thing that upset me most was the attitude of many in the community. With a few exceptions, most seemed to be indifferent to our plight. During the last weeks before we were deported and sent off to Auschwitz, nobody protested against the way we were mistreated. Now that the war had been over for many months and so few of us survived and came back, I had hoped to find a more sympathetic reception.

I had the impression that we had no right to come back and disturb their memory with our presence.

As days and weeks passed, my loneliness grew. My family, my mother and father, my sister and brother, my grandmother, I missed them terribly.

My cousins Ibi and Laicsi, two out of ten siblings, had survived, the other eight and their parents, my aunt and uncle Markovich from Zalau have not. My uncle Kibovics the watchmaker from Oradea survived, his wife, my father's sister, and their two children did not. My uncle Chaim Mandel, my mother's brother, and their son, my cousin, had not; all my Jewish schoolmates, including their families, did not return.

Now there was the former Ghetto, about a little over a Km. Outside the City limits. As a Jewish teenager I should have known more about Ghettos. The name Ghetto was rarely used in this context in our community. Before the war Jews of Transylvania and Hungary were well integrated. In the middle ages in Catholic dominated countries of Europe such as Italy, Jews were required to live separately; I believe the name Ghetto is of Italian origin.

I still remember the hillside Ghetto imposed on us before deportation. That hill was well known for the endless fruit orchards that graced it. In early summer of 1945, after I returned home some weeks had passed. I was thinking about going there with someone but with whom? Then I thought it would be best if I went alone. My memories of that place were too fresh; last year we were thousands, whole families trapped behind a barbed wire fence and guarded by armed Hungarian Fascists all volunteers. I decided I'd go by myself to visit this hollowed ground; its significance would only be diluted by the presents of others.

Then it all became clearer. Why should I want to revisit that nightmare? It was an enormous crime scene: crimes committed against my family and all the Jewish inhabitants of my town. To visit this former prison without walls, it was too painful to contemplate. It was only a year ago that we were literally herded onto that hillside.

There my parents, my old grandmother, Rifku my sister, my cousin Ibi, and I and all the other many families, spent our last days and nights in mortal fear, all trapped and abandoned to the murderous Hungarian Fascist thugs.

The few male returnees were young men a few years older than I. They had served in labor brigades for the Hungarian army. When they were overrun and liberated by the advancing Soviet Army, they were among the first to return. Although the communists ruled Romania the country appeared to be prospering. By the time we started to trickle back from the camps life in the city was near normal. Bistrita was now a magnet for people from the surrounding towns and from the other side of the Carpathian Mountains; from Chernovitz-Bucovina many found Bistrita a pleasant city to live in.

I had a surprise visit from Vasile. I was glad to see him. Vasile was an apprentice in my father's shop; the two of us had not changed much visibly. We were fond of each other. Without hesitation, he pulled out the wristwatch I had tossed to him from the truck the morning we were removed from our home. He offered it back to me and said; "Do you remember? My answer was; "Of course I do, I really want you to have this watch, please keep it it's yours. A year ago, you were there for us, you were the only one, who shared in our grief, I'll always remember you" After fifty and some years I often think of Vasile and wonder if he had a good life. I hope he did, and thinks of me also sometimes.

My half sister Rozsi, whom I had not seen for so many years, was back in town. I was told she was married to Emanuel Moskovitsh. I was given her address, but I made no attempt to see her. My childhood indoctrination kept me away. To see her would have been some kind of betrayal of my mother's wishes. I wrestled with that thought, I had to think about it. In hind sight my behavior was absolutely inexcusable and wrong.

Before we were deported my father's store had an inventory of hundreds of pairs of shoes, and a large inventory of upper and sole leather materials. Although our home was vandalized, my father's store in the center of town stayed locked down for many months, until September of 1944, when Bistrita was liberated by the Russian Army.

On the main street of Bistrita the large cooperative had a retail store. It sold merchandise of every description; clothing, shoes, fabrics by the yard, glass and pottery. It was the best going retail business in town, called "Cooperativa" On a visit to the store I discovered that a large part of the inventory was taken from stores and businesses whose Jewish owners had not returned and from businesses that the Germans (Saxons) had abandoned before the Russians arrived. Stolen merchandise.

I could rationalize the looting from the enemy, but I could not understand why they would break into Jewish owned homes and businesses, months before the war had ended. Instead of protecting those properties, they broke into them and stole the contents. I also discovered that shoes from my father's store were on the shelves and even on display in the store's front windows. I confronted those who should have known and told them that the footwear on display belonged to my father, and since he had not returned yet to claim his property, the goods rightfully belonged to me. Through a conspiracy of silence they ignored me completely. The "Cooperativa" was managed by a group of self appointed guardians. A group of individuals claiming to protect the abandoned and so far unclaimed property, but behind it all, they were a bunch of thieves accounting to nobody.

The city had no impartial authority in place. The Soviets were in charge of security, and an imposed night curfew was strictly enforced; anyone caught after midnight was arrested and held at the Commandatura until morning. All official matters were handled by and through the all powerful Communist party, an ideology I never liked or fully understood. To claim rights to property seemed absurd at the time. Had I initiated a claim for the goods that were stolen from my fathers business, it would have taken months, maybe years, to have the claim adjudicated, and certainly without a guarantee to a favorable outcome.

The city government had changed and the population changed considerably. The Saxons who supported Hitler's causes, in fear of retribution, left with the retreating German Armies. They left their farms; the best stores and homes were now abandoned. From the surrounding villages the Romanians moved into the former Saxon homes and worked the farms as their own.

My friends, the Lowy brothers, Simon and Herman, were also liberated in Ebensee. They also returned to Bistrita and moved into a second floor apartment at the Piata Mica (small market square). As for me, since I was unhappy living alone in my parent's house, I invited myself and moved in with my friends and shared the expenses. There is more to Simon than I have written so far. He is more than a friend. Before deportation I knew of Simon that was all. I began to observe Simon in Melk (concentration camp) and for the first time I had the good fortune to experience his unselfish behavior to observe his joy of living even under those conditions, a rare quality to emanate from a young man who had possibly not finished grade school, but had a sense of humanity not to be found in the educated of that day. After all these years he never knew how I used to cling to every expression of his.

Simon and his wife Sidy live in NY City. From time to time I call him, I enjoy our conversations. We touch on certain episodes we experienced in camp. I think it pains him more than it hurts me to remember events from camp. He does not want to be the big brother any more. When I began collecting notes for my memoir I called Simon to affirm a particular event we both experienced, participated. Instead to acknowledge the happening he began to cry . . . and said, "I'm sorry, I can't remember" That in itself is an involuntary life saving mechanism. I think it is better to forget than to remember those horrible events we both lived through.

Many would say now, how great you remember such and such . . . It's a curse to carry a heavy load of memories that can show up any time unannounced and in nightmares.

Now sharing the apartment with the Lowy brothers. life was more bearable there, it was lively we made new friends, we always had overnight visitors. Simon prepared good meals, I don't know when, but he learned how to cook; all who visited had something good to eat. He'd be surprised to know that I still remember the delicious roasted lamb he prepared. To have a four to six egg omelet each for breakfast was normal. My favorite was an open sandwich, a large slice of home baked bread with butter and honey spread thick on top.

From the apartment we could look down on the market place. Compared to the large market that took place every Tuesday, this was in a small area just off the center of town called Piata Mica. Twice a week, Sundays and Fridays, small farmers and vegetable growers from the surrounding villages came to sell their fresh produce.

On Sundays, by midday vendors had to pack up their unsold produce and leave the market square, after they left, the area was swept clean. One event stands out above others. On that Sunday I had been to my parents' house for a short visit. Even though no one lived there, I often went there; walking through the empty rooms was my way of staying in touch with my family, I could sense their presence better that way. On my way back, I came upon a Romanian man who carried in his arms a small black lamb with a white nose. The lamb was for sale at such a ridiculously low price I couldn't resist and bought it. When Simon saw the lamb in my arms he asked: "What are you doing? Why did you take the lamb out of the shed?" I told him I had just bought it from a man who didn't want to take it back to his village. He sold it to me at a very low price. Simon led me to the shed to show me the lamb he had bought a couple of hours before. The shed was empty, evidently the man who sold him the lamb and put it in the shed, came back later and took (stole) the lamb he had sold Simon earlier.

Over the years we sometimes remember the episode of:

"The lamb we bought and paid for twice"

The apartment was a hangout for many who needed a temporary place to stay. Socially we soon had an enlarged group of friends: Mendi, Shmilku Harnick, Alex Landesman, the Shpitz sisters, Henyu, Simi and Mutza the youngest; Margo, Rifku, Hedy Pasternak and others whose names I can't remember. We became close friends and inseparable. We all had returned from concentration camps except Margo and Alex. Margo Blau was born in Mexico, I don't know much about her background, but I do know she was not in any of the Nazi camps. During the war Alex was a partisan whose guerrilla tactics against the Germans were effective. By blowing up bridges and rail lines, they slowed down considerably the shipments of German troops and war materials to the front. Alex was the only survivor in his family. Before the war Alex's father had a sewing machine shop and his mother and my mother knew each other well. Margo and Alex were soon married. Rifcu had a crush on Shmilku Harnick but for some reason they did not make it together. Shmilku emigrated to Israel; Rifku eventually emigrated to the U.S. I thought I liked Hedy but she lacked a precious commodity, a sense of humor. Since we had so little else in common, interest in each other cooled to a chill. Simi was lovely and bright, she was exceptional; the most thoughtful and reflective, she was the darling among us.

Simi survived the Stuthoff concentration camp, in spite of extreme hardships during the winter of 1944/45 with severely frost bitten toes of both her feet. Although she never complained, I was sure she was in constant pain. The three Shpitz sisters survived and returned home. Their mother and father and other siblings were killed in Auschwitz. Before our deportation Simi's father was a candy maker, He specialized in making hard candy which came in many colors and flavors. The house they lived in before the war was on the Magyar Street next to the Magjaros Rabbi's small synagogue, to which my father belonged.

Then the Shpitz sisters had moved into a house that belonged to a relative whose family also did not return from the camps. It was understandable that they did not want to stay in the same apartment they lived in before deportation. In my parents' house the walls still echoed with their voices; we all needed the companionship of others.

One day in late August, I met a man who was a survivor of Mauthausen who told me that he had seen my father a week before liberation, he also alerted me about a death march to or from Gusen, a satellite camp of Mauthausen that took place about that time. Others who knew my father suggested that I should think about opening a shoe shop since it would be a good idea to get something started in case he returned; I still had not given up all hope.

Mr. Lauber the local tanner invited me to visit his tannery to look over his inventory of leathers; he also offered me a substantial line of credit. The tannery was on a road outside the city limits. To get there I had to pass by the store and house where my half sister Rozsi lived. On a return from one of those visits, it seemed as though Rozsi was waiting for me. I could not avoid her any longer. She stopped me in the street and said, "Why do you avoid me? Isn't Papy my father also? This was the first time I heard her call our father Papy. In the past when we were children she always called him Papa. (dad in Hungarian) "Whatever you do or think you'll always be my little brother" That wall between us began to crumble, I could not keep that prejudicial distance between us anymore. I could not hold back my tears, I was speechless. All I could do was embrace her. She invited me into her home where we talked about all the years that had separated us.

She told me that she always kept herself informed about us; after all, we were her family. She was reluctant to talk about herself then, but invited me to dinner the next Friday night. I was eager to meet her new spouse and learn more about her and her two boys, my younger nephews, who were shunned by my mother because their father was not Jewish by birth.

The Friday night dinner went well. The Shabbat table was set, a chalah covered with an embroidered cloth. Sabbath candles shone brightly, the meal was delicious. The Friday night home atmosphere was a reminder of how it used to be before I was so brutally taken from my home. I missed my family; in my thoughts they were still in the present. To speak of them in a past tense was as if placing them at too far a distance.

I had gone to the dinner on my bicycle carrying a bottle of wine in my left hand while steering with my right hand only. Getting off the sidewalk curb, I lost my balance and fell on my left knee, still holding on to the bottle. I had a clear choice, let the bottle fall and break, or fall on my knee and save the bottle of wine. I chose unwisely; two days later my friends had to take me to the hospital. My knee had swelled from an internal hemorrhage and I had a high fever and was in much pain. Before the doctor lanced my knee I was given laughing gas. Throughout the procedure Simon and Herman were at my side. After it was over they wanted to know what I had dreamt about, they had never seen me so happy and laugh so hard they said. A few days later I was well again. Had anything like that happened to me in concentration camp, an injury followed by an infection, it would have resulted in certain death.

Mendi, my half sister Rozsi's husband, was a friendly man. He listened to me intently, he told me about his own personal experiences during the war. Rozsi was

115

happy for me, to have survived and come home. From then on I often visited with my new found family.

Mendi operated a small general merchandise store. It was stocked with all kinds of grocery items; rice, potatoes, beans, sugar, salt, cooking oil, vinegar, fresh vegetables, kerosene for lamps, fly paper, tobacco, cigarettes and many other household items. After each visit he always gave me a packet of a hundred 'National' brand cigarettes. Cigarettes were sold by the piece also. I was never without cigarettes, I shared them with my friends. I had more cigarettes than I wanted to smoke. My addiction to cigarettes may have begun then.

As for Rozsi, I knew I had to wait for the right moment when she would be ready to talk about herself. There was sadness about her it was very painful for her. Then finally one day we had a long talk, she began to pour her heart out.

During the war, Cocon, the father of her boys, her first husband she eloped with and gave up her family, had served in the Hungarian army. In the town where they lived, their family was not discriminated against, as other Jews were, but she always feared for herself and the children. The night before all Jews were forcibly taken from their homes, she was forewarned by a town official who advised her to leave and she managed to escape.

Pretending to be an uprooted Romanian family from Hungary, she and her young boys (my nephews) Ernest and Mihai, crossed the border into Romania, there they were placed in a camp for Romanian refugees from Hungary.

Five months later, in the fall of 1944, the Romanians quit the Axis (the alliance with Germany). The Russians liberated occupied Transylvania, and all the refugees could return to their homes. On her return to Lechinta the town they lived in before the war, she found her husband already there with another woman. He rejected my sister, he was abusive to her; he absolutely wanted to free himself from her. Under some pretense he took the boys away from her and placed them with his mother and his family.

My sister was devastated; after all she had been through to save herself and her two boys. They were now taken away from her: She had no one to turn to for help.

In October of 1944, the war in Transylvania was over, but it was still raging in Western Europe and the outcome was still in doubt. In that small town it was very difficult for her to survive. Mendi was among the first Jewish returnees from the Hungarian labor brigades. They found comfort in each other, together they moved to Bistrita. Every attempt she made to find and get her children back was blocked by Cocon, and made more difficult. When the war ended and survivors began to trickle back, her hopes rose that the time had come for her to get legitimate custody of her children.

1945 what a year that was; from days filled with suffering, hopelessness and fear, to days of hope. I was 19, others in our group were between 16 and 22 years old. Without parents, we needed each other's friendship and guidance. We grew fond of each other, some paired up, married and started new. We no longer had to fear for our lives, Nazi Germany was defeated, the feared Nazi youth gangs in their brown shirts were no more. Only my own haunting fears and bad memories were a constant reminder. Often my dreams turned into nightmares. I always ended up looking for my father; the dream was always the same or with slight variations. Walking in a crowded city street looking ahead, seeing my father, running to catch up with the person who appeared to be my father, then coming closer, almost bumping into the person, then apologizing for my mistake. Over many months I continued to have the same recurring dreams, they were so real. Other times I was back in concentration camp wondering how stupid of me to be so helpless and careless to let the Nazis get me again, then waking exhausted and frightened.

Simi's house was centrally located, we often met there. We all got along well, we planned our activities together. We went on excursions on foot or on bicycles, we discovered country roads and villages we had not seen or visited before. We had parties often; on an old victorola we played records of popular Hungarian and Romanian songs. On weekends we went to the movies; the Arthur Rank British films and American westerns were popular. English sounds seemed strange with words like "how—now—wow" The language was very strange, but I hoped that one day soon I'd be able to understand, speak and read English.

One late afternoon in November when the first snow fell, we hired a horse drawn sled. The driver gave us warm blankets to bundle up in, we sang, we laughed, we were happy. With sleigh bells ringing, we were driven in all directions, far beyond the city limits, an experience I never had before. It had been snowing all day, huge white snowflakes covered everything, and all the black and other shades of gray in between turned white. A pure white as if painted with a celestial brush. The slightest incline was quickly populated with children pulling sleds, playing, laughing, throwing snowballs, and rolling in the white fluffy cotton. The view was incomplete, no Jewish children among them playing in the snow, their lives had been snuffed out two springs ago. I labored hard not to betray my thoughts, the snow was forgiving, and it covered all imperfections in the landscape, an unforgettable experience.

The Sugalete is a 16Th century arched walkway, under a dozen or more buildings in the center of town; similar to the arcaded walks in other European cities. The stores under the arches were favorite meeting places especially in winter. Under the arches vendors sold freshly roasted chestnuts; a bag of hot chestnuts kept our hands warm while we socialized, walking under the Sugalete. All along the Sugalete there were the taxi stands and a number of horse drawn carriages. Taxis were used for out-of-town rides, horse drawn carriages for shorter trips or to the rail station.

As the days and weeks passed, the summer of 1946 was nearly over; we realized that this euphoria, that carefree aimless existence could not last for long. We had to think about our futures. Margo and Alex got married, Hedy moved to Bucharest to live with relatives, Simi decided to go to Cluj, and planned to enroll in school that fall and she did. Simon and Herman also planned to leave, leave the country but didn't know when. I also had to decide what to do.

Fellow survivors from Bistrita. Taken in Bistrita 1946 I'm 2nd from right.

Fellow survivors from Bistrita. Heidi,me & Simi

Chapter 9

GOING TO AMERICA

I corresponded regularly with my aunt in America. In each letter she urged me to leave, leave the town, leave the country and go to a displaced persons camp in the American occupied zone of Germany. It was impossible to emigrate legally from Romania to America. Ironically, I'd be safer in West Germany than staying in a Communist country. Others had the same idea. My friends, Simon and Herman, for fear of being drafted into the Romanian army, they left for Germany, hoping that from there they would be able to go to America.

Time flew by, the summer was over. We were teenagers with no one to guide us. Our education had been interrupted a few years earlier. In real life experiences, we had matured much sooner than we wished. To finish high school and further our education that was interrupted, was a future we wanted for ourselves. It was near the end of August 1946, by now our group that was so inseparable, was coming apart. I also had to decide. Had I stayed I would have been drafted into the Romanian military. I gave up the idea of starting a shoe business and decided to postpone going back to school. I had to save myself. My parents' property was not going to decide my future; I decided to leave everything.

I had one last good visit with my half sister, it was not easy to be separated again; we were not to see each other for more than 20 years. With a few things packed in a rucksack, the same one I arrived with the year before, I boarded a train headed in the direction of the Hungarian border. On the way I wanted, I had to make a few stops.

My first stop was Dej. I had to visit my father's cousin Martin, whom I had not seen since we were liberated in Ebensee. We spent a pleasant evening together, we were glad to see each other again. The year before while in Ebensee KZ camp he was so optimistic about survival and the future, now he vas a broken man he too was a lone survivor, his wife and children were gassed in Auschwitz. He also did not want to stay in Romania, eventually he hoped to go to Palestine. I spent the night in his place, he thought it was wise of me to leave Romania.

My next stop was Cluj, 30 kilometers from Dej. I very much wanted to see Simi one more time. Cluj, the capital of Transylvania, was a large city with a population over 100,000, with good schools and fine institutions, and well known for its commerce and trade. Originally the city was established on a site of an ancient Roman settlement.

Simi lived in a dormitory for girls. I had a hard time finding her address.

I hoped I could persuade her to come with me. Simi was glad to see me, she looked well and seemed to be happy. We walked, we talked we spent a few hours together my reasons for leaving were not good enough for her. I offered to stay and wait for her. She told me she was comfortable in her situation. She had new friends and looked forward to continuing her education, and Cluj had so much to offer. It was early afternoon; the day was very hot, and she was visibly hurried. I admit I was disappointed that Simi had other plans. I had looked forward to seeing her, she was my friend—I loved her. Weeks had passed since she left our town. During those weeks I had no contact with her and I missed her very much. The friendships and the people I was close to, slowly vanished. However disillusioned and unhappy I was, there was no turning back for me. We said goodbye, and I took a late afternoon train that headed for the Hungarian border.

Once on the moving train, it all became clear somehow that although we liked each other a lot, we saw different futures for ourselves. Simi's future was set on its course in Romania; as for me, my future was in a long journey that was uncertain and difficult at times. On the train were others whose aim was similar to mine. We wanted to cross into Hungary. For many months after the war the borders were open, people could travel in both directions. Thousands of refugees crossed daily by any means possible; now the border was jealously guarded. We got off the train at a town just before the border, then one by one we walked to a nearby village. Although this was Romanian territory, everyone spoke Hungarian. We soon learned that crossing borders illegally was a special industry.

We didn't have to look for guides, they found us; for a price, sooner or later we'd cross over the border. In small groups of three or four we were placed in different shelters for that night and the next day. For a few extra dollars we were sure not to be betrayed. For food and shelter we paid in Romanian currency. I spent all the Lei (Romanian money) I had. Anyway the Leu was worthless in Hungary.

Lodging for the night and next day we paid ten dollars per person. We feared they would keep us there longer than they had promised. Next day before evening set in, the guide told us about a wedding that would take place. I still wonder whether the wedding was real or staged for our benefit.

At the end of the war, the border, arbitrarily divided the farmlands and the families who lived on them. This resulted in farmlands in Romania with the families who owned them living in Hungary, and vice versa. We were told that the wedding would take place on both sides of the border. Besides the bride and groom, relatives, friends and guests will be at the wedding. We were to mix with the natives and act the part. We were also told that we will cross the border on oxcarts, we'll be given bouquets of flowers to carry and banners to wave, we should sing; we should participate as wedding guests.

Since we all spoke Hungarian it was easy to play the part. The event was lively and the bribed border guards were accommodating. From a village on the other side of the border, we were then taken to a town with a train station; then with the next train we went to Budapest. The border authorities were strict to the limit of their greed in extracting cash payments for their cooperation.

The train was slow with many stops along the way. To be less conspicuous we settled into different compartments. Doubt and feelings of regret were in my thoughts; maybe I made a mistake leaving my home town and all I was familiar with. I had about two hundred dollars in twenty and ten dollar bills; money my aunt Rose in America had sent me over a period of months. It was a considerable sum and so far I had not spent much. I wondered how long my money would last.

About noon the train pulled into Budapest. In the station there were many young men and women, survivors of concentration camps. They came from all parts of Hungary and Transylvania, they also found no purpose remaining in the towns and villages they lived in before the war. As we came off the trains, agents of the J.D.C. (Joint Distribution Committee an American aid organization) helped us find our way to the shelters they provided for us, to rest up and get a warm meal.

The designated places were old hotels that were infested with bedbugs. Those little creatures appeared from their hiding places only in the dark. The room I shared with many others had a single light bulb hanging from the ceiling, which was never turned off. (Déjà vu, I've been here before) I am not critical of our hosts on the contrary I was grateful for the accommodations that were warmly provided. It was well known then, that many of the old buildings were infested with bedbugs. Most who stopped here, including myself, only stayed a few days. Ironically, just a little over a year before, I passed through here with high hopes, eager to go home and be reunited with my parents, and be a family again.

I remember how energized most of us were then, willing to forgive all, just to be back and start over again. How innocent and naive I was. Now I was tired of going from place to place.

I feared to be stateless and homeless. I knew I was walking a thin line, at any moment I could have fallen to the other side of sanity. It has been said that the homeless are mentally unstable, and that's why they are homeless. I believe a homeless person without hope can't possibly remain sane for long.

I remember I did not stay long at the shelter; in a day or so I joined a group whose aim was to cross the border into Austria and then ultimately to Vienna. We studied train schedules to Sopron, a border town in Hungary; there we had an address where to meet.

Upon arriving to Sopron I looked out of my compartment window. It was a small rail station. Just off the main platform I observed men in civilian clothes randomly checking I.D. cards of passengers. This being a border town it was not unusual but, having come from Romania, and without proper documentation, I tried to avoid being detained. Passengers in my compartment were preparing to get off. A woman with two young children and with a few pieces of luggage was getting ready to leave; I offered to help her carry a child and a piece of luggage. We exited together without a problem.

Nobody was waiting for her at the station, she thanked me and I was on my way. Shopron, this town on the border with Austria was small; any passing strangers on Main Street would have been noticed. Only once did I ask for direction to the address were we were to meet. In this border town any stranger could be suspect. I certainly did not want to be detained by the border police.

The meeting place was a small private house at the edge of town with a large garden with a fenced-in yard. We spent the night in a large room in the attic, we paid the equivalent of ten dollars each, and for food we paid extra.

Ten dollars was too much for a cot in a room with fifteen others, but we had no choice. Our host was the contact man with the guide who would walk us across the border.

Next day we were told that the guide will arrive before sunset, and those who wished to cross the border should meet with him at the edge of the vineyard a short distance from the house. The weather was good all day but late in the afternoon the sky was covered with dark rain clouds. We waited for the guide whom we had not met before. Finally he arrived and in a low voice gave us instructions how to follow him through the forest, which was just ahead. He told us to be absolutely quiet and promised, that for 20 US dollars per person he would guide us safely across the border. Had we met him earlier we probably would not have trusted him. He didn't look trustworthy but it was too late, we had to take a chance with him.

After he collected his fee from all, we started out through the forest toward the border. By then heavy clouds covered the sky. We followed the guide in single file touching the shoulder of the person in front. We could hear thunder in the distance. The darkness became so complete I could not see the person in front of me. Walking this way took us much longer than the guide anticipated.

At one point we stopped abruptly. A little ahead we could hear the Austrian border guards' voices, and could see the beams from their flashlights. They were not walking towards us, they appeared to be going in a direction from left to right. After a short pause we continued. The guide took us well past the border into Austria, all the way to the edge of the forest. There he pointed to electric lights and to the town we would descend to, and instructed us to take the first train of the day out. He assured us we would have no trouble, only mail and freight from the local factory would be on the first train at 5 a.m.

He also gave us approximate directions to the train station. Once we reached the village we'd see the station to our left.

The guide left us about two hours after midnight; then shortly after it started to rain.

Most of us had some kind of rainwear I had a long black rubberized coat, much too large for me, but for this occasion it was great. I covered my head and shoulders and found a rock to sit on; it rained hard on and off.

I was very tired, even though I was sitting on a jagged rock I had a restful sleep for about two hours. Unaware when the rain had stopped, I awoke feeling good and refreshed, the air was damp and the sky was dotted with stars.

We began to plan our next move. Without a paved road to the village, we decided to cross the field in front of us; we did not count on the deep mud we had to track through. By the time we reached the village we were exhausted. We scraped the mud off our boots the best we could, then headed toward the train station.

A train was about to leave. We jumped on it as it began to move, and we separated into different compartments. It wasn't long before we stopped at the next station. There a number of young Austrians and four Russian soldiers came on board. The Austrians began to heckle us; we understood what they were saying. They were rude they must have sensed that we had just crossed the border; In the meantime a few of the boys from our group who spoke Russian had a good time with the young soldiers, one told them how nasty the Austrians were to us. The Russian soldiers jumped to their feet, used a few familiar curse words and chased the Austrians from our compartment and threatened to throw them off the moving train if they showed their faces again.

Austrians or Germans, I disliked them equally. I considered them all to be Nazis. In the camps some Austrians were crueler than the Germans. After all, how could we forget that both Hitler and Eichmann were Austrian.

Adolf Eichmann, this notorious minor official in the Nazi party, was assigned the task to gather and transport all the Jews of Hungary to Auschwitz.

From March to May of 1944, various attempts had been made to slow down the deportations, but by the middle of May the trainloads of sealed cattle cars to Auschwitz kept on rolling without interruption. I promised myself not to engage in statistics here, but there are those who claim that not enough was done by those who were in the position to negotiate, to ransom the lives of hundreds of thousands although some, not many lives were saved.

After the Austrians left our compartment we had a good laugh, and that changed the mood for all of us. As for train tickets, again no one bothered us about them.

More than a year after the war Austria was still full of refugees. People of many nationalities, train loads of Austrian and German prisoners of war newly released, mainly from the Soviet Union, were all going somewhere.

In Vienna we checked into the Rothschild Hotel. I hardly remember the hotel, except for the untold thousands of displaced people who passed through daily. It was a welcome place to rest for a few days, and a meeting place for those who went ahead or fell behind in travel.

A year earlier, on my way home, when I first came through Vienna, the effects of the war were visible everywhere. Entire sections of the city were flattened; it appeared like a huge ghost city. Now, a year later, the heaps of rubble were removed; the electric street cars, though very crowded, were running on schedule.

Compared to a year ago life appeared normal, but the people in the street were just as unfriendly as ever. I could hear their nasty remarks about the "Auslander" (foreigners).

They did not know that this Auslander understood German. It's been a long year since I passed through Vienna after liberation. I was never a vengeful person, I hate conflict of any kind. These former Nazis, I liked them better right after the war, when they were hungry, many homeless, beaten down. Clearly they have not learned much from the war. They had not changed, they still had an inborn hatred toward all who were not Aryan.

That became more evident many years later when Kurt Waldheim the former Secretary General of the United Nations 1972-1981 was exposed to the world as having been a Nazi officer who behaved criminally during the war while stationed in Yugoslavia and Greece. After having been publicly disgraced, in 1986 the Austrians elected him as their President.

For decades after the war the Austrians believed in their own fabricated myth that they were the first victims of Hitler's aggression. It took them 60 years after the war to recognize that Hitler was Austrian and to their willing complicity with the Third Reich.

I still do not understand how it was possible for Mr. Waldheim (a former Nazi) to have been nominated and elected as Secretary General of the United Nations. I often wonder how many other former Nazi criminals live out their lives in relative safety in different parts of the world.

I had no time to waste on the Austrians, I did not trust them. I was determined to go to Germany and find the displaced persons camp where my friends the Lowy brothers were. Traveling by train was not too difficult as long as you could tolerate the crowded conditions. It made no difference day or night the trains were congested far above capacity. I traveled light, all my belongings were in a rucksack. The little food I brought from Vienna I had eaten long ago. The station restaurants had nothing to offer: bread and basic food items were scarce and available only through ration coupons. To receive coupons one had to have had an established address. If you had the time to find a gasthaus (restaurant) away from the crowded train station you could get a bowl of hot kimmel soup without a ration coupon, and an occasional weak beer on tap. I was more preoccupied with being on schedule.

Some trains were so overcrowded that it was impossible to get on them. The time between train connections gave me an opportunity to seek out a gasthaus for soup.

The natives very much resented the Auslander for buying the very little that was available for sale. My train ran along the Danube towards Linz. One of the stops was in Melk. Outside this city less then 1 Km. From this station, I had spent ten months in a KZ labor camp. In Melk I had struggled to survive, not only from hunger, physical abuse and hard labor, but also to endure all the indignities and mental tortures that were inflicted upon us daily. All the time we were made to feel that we were less than human, and did not deserve to live. I still shudder when Melk is mentioned; there I was separated from my father, never to see him again.

What strength need one have to be able to put aside such unendurable hurt and believe in oneself and not give up?

Professor Avram my history teacher in high school taught us ancient history in an eloquent way. He once said: Names, places and dates were important, but most import were the lessons we must derive from those great events, long past and some forgotten in human history. The might of those empires and their rulers did not and could not endure for long, because they enslaved the people they conquered. I never missed a lecture of his. I often think of Professor Avram and how fortunate I was to have had such a fine teacher.

The dreaded Mauthausen concentration camp was not far from Melk.

Simon Wiesenthal was liberated from Mauthausen. We owe him much gratitude. Through his tireless efforts his organization succeeded in finding and arresting Nazis including the police officer that was responsible for the deportation of Anne Frank and her family. Simon Wiesenthal is a man who dedicated his life to hunt down Nazi war criminals wherever they may hide. From humble beginnings his organization is now known as the most effective in bringing Nazi war criminals to justice. After over half a century that work is still ongoing.

From Melk the train went to Linz, then to Passau on the German border. There the M.P.'s (American Military Police) were helpful. They guided us to an U.N.R.R.A. (United Nations Refugee Relief Agency) aid station.

After the war, the United Nations established a D.P. camp system for displaced persons that would house and feed the many thousands of homeless refugees. Some camps were for orphaned children only, with hospitals to care for the sick. How ironic that Germany, that cursed place, would become the country in which future generations of Jews would be shaped and born again, in a few short years.

After a short interview we were taken by train to a D.P. camp. Its population was housed in US Army tents, lined up in long rows on an open field with small spaces between them. My tent had ten army field cots. By the time we settled in, it was near supper time. I was hungry and tired; I enjoyed the meal and went to sleep early. During the night it rained but the ground under the tent stayed dry. At daybreak I looked outside and saw that the road between the tents had become a sea of mud. I went back to my cot and slept soundly, only to wake when I heard a familiar voice calling "Jankov Hersh" "Jankov Hersh". The closer the voice came the clearer and more familiar it became. I stepped out to see the person whose voice I heard. To my surprise it was Sheindi Kaufteil, a young woman from my home town, who had come to find her cousin. We spoke briefly, we were surprised to find each other that way. She continued her search, then came back a short time later. Sadly she did not find her cousin.

We talked for a while. She wanted to know what my plans were. She told me that she and her sister and a number of others from Bistrita were in a D.P. camp in Ulm, a couple of hours by train from Munich, and if I wanted I could go with her. I was buoyed by the opportunity and the sheer excitement of meeting someone I knew in such an unlikely place.

I picked up my belongings and we quickly left the camp and boarded a train towards Munich, then to Augsburg, and finally to Ulm. We traveled practically all day.

I was welcomed by my landsmen (compatriots). That was exactly what I needed to be lifted out of my depression; I was welcomed like a brother. Among others there were

Gershon Fogel and his sister; before the war they were a family of five children. Their father had a soda factory on Beitler Street, a store front with a few tables and chairs and the bottling enterprise in the back of the store. I recall the many times in summer days, I used to stop in for a bottle of soda. The pint size bottle had a solid glass sphere the size of a large marble suspended in the pinched neck of the bottle, which kept the fizz from escaping. This sweet soda came in many candy shades.

The Fogels and the Kaufteils were exceptionally nice to me. Gershon remembered my brother Bumi (Avrum.) We remembered and mourned those who meant so much to us and never returned.

With all the warmth and comfort offered to me, I still felt out of place. They expressed deep religious beliefs: that God will punish our oppressors and in time we will be redeemed. With such a strong fundamental faith their emotional healing was well on the way.

I envied them, I couldn't and didn't express my feelings to them. As for me my religious beliefs had been on a downward slide. How could an Almighty God, a God we believed in, a God who shelters the innocent and punishes the wicked and the cruel, exist? It's pointless to believe that such a God would groom a new Pharaoh (Hitler) to lead a people of willing executioners who in twelve years of madness would systematically murder eleven million people, among them six million Jews; innocent men, women and children. What sins could innocent children have committed to deserve such a cruel fate? Nazi Germany almost succeeded in killing all the Jews of Europe; for the few of us who survived, what kind of redemption can we expect? We will never be as we were. To be made whole again? . . . I knew that was impossible.

I stayed in Ulm for the Rosh Hashanah holiday. I did not want to stay there longer. During that week I found out that my friends the Lowy brothers, Simon and Herman, were in a D.P. camp in Windsheim. After the holidays I thanked my hosts for their warm hospitality and left. I had no idea where Windsheim was. On a map I located the town between Wurzburg and Furth in Bavaria, a direct line to Nuremberg. The train ride to Wurzburg took about half a day. As usual the trains were overcrowded, people were standing on steps, between wagons, holding on to whatever possible.

In Wurzburg I had to wait a couple of hours for my connection to Neustadt and Furth, with Windsheim in between. In a short time I learned a lot about the German rail system. Not far from the train station the devastation from allied bombing was great. As far as the eye could see entire sections of the city were leveled to the ground. It had been said that among Bavarian cities, Wurzburg was bombed the heaviest.

The streets were barely passable; occasionally a man on a bicycle found his way zigzagging through the rubble. Seeing all that destruction, I felt an empty kind of satisfaction. Although the Germans brought that ruin upon themselves, I was sure there were innocent victims among them. In Wurzburg, while I was waiting for my train connection, a long awaited announcement about the Nazi war crimes trial at Nuremberg came on the station's loudspeaker.

THE NUREMBERG War Crimes TRIAL, The International Military Tribunal tried twenty-two of Nazi Germany's political leaders. The judgment was delivered on September 30, and on October 1, 1946. Twelve were sentenced to death; Bormann was not captured, Goering committed suicide in his cell, the other ten were to be hanged on Oct. 6, 1946.

Nuremberg, that infamous city, where Nazi laws against humanity and against Jews in particular were passed. It was fitting that the war time trials against the Nazi leadership were held there.

From Wurzburg the train cut across northern Bavaria. Before arriving at the Windsheim station, the tracks ran right through the D.P. camp. Because of the heavy foot traffic across the rail tracks, the train always slowed down to a crawl; that made it possible for the camp dwellers to jump off the moving train. The station was just about half a kilometer from the camp.

For the next three years the Displaced Persons Camp in Windsheim was to become my home. It was a large garden type housing development. During the war the buildings housed both civilian and German military personnel and their families. Each building with separate entrances, housed two families.

The houses were set back from the street. There were no sidewalks except for a narrow cement walk from the street to the entrance of each house. All the houses were of the same design, each consisted of two rooms and a kitchen, with a room in the attic with a separate entrance from the side of the house.

Windsheim is a medieval city with narrow cobblestone streets, all emanating from the Gothic City Hall at its center. It was also known for its summer resorts with Kurhaus (health spa) buildings located in a beautiful wooded area. Those buildings housed the U.N.R.R.A. camp administration and supply warehouses.

My friends the Lowy brothers shared a house with the Pollaks, a married couple. The larger bedroom was the couple's, Simon, Herman and two other young men occupied the first room; for beds we had US Army cots. The kitchen facility was shared by all. The rooms had no furniture or closets, extra clothes were hung from nails in the wall.

To become a resident, first I had to find a place to stay. Because the turnover was small vacancies were hard to find. I was welcomed to stay with Simon and Herman; now we were five in one small room.

Since I left Romania, for the first time I felt secure with friends with a special bond between us. We cared for each other like brothers. At times the open cots covered most of the floor space of our room. The married couple had to climb over the cots before they could reach the door to their room, but we managed amazingly well. The camp provided housing, food rations, or one could go to the communal dining room for meals. The camp had an internal police force, a trash collection brigade and a flourishing mini black market.

After I established myself with my new address, I resumed the long neglected correspondence with my aunt in America. She began to look into possible ways for me to emigrate. She sent me "Care" packages (those wonderful packages that contained

127

food stuffs that were impossible to buy not even on the black market) followed by letters with ten or twenty dollar bills tucked away between the pages.

The DP camp population possibly outnumbered the townspeople. Over time I got to know several German families, in particular the Gottvalds; my ability to converse in German made that possible. I found it incredible how much they blamed one person, Hitler, for all that happened to them, how conveniently they excluded themselves from responsibility (guilt).

In all my conversations with them, not once did anyone express regret or sorrow for what they, as a nation, a people, had inflicted on the world. They blamed everything on the war and Hitler.

The camp population was mostly Jewish from Poland and Russia, and some not many from Hungary, Rumania and Czechoslovakia. The non-Jews were from Poland and the Ukraine. For the first time after the war, I saw Polish Jewish families, whole families, mothers, fathers, small children, grandparents, and old men with long white beards, families that had never been separated.

The Non Aggression pact between Nazi Germany and the Soviet Union also divided Poland in two. The Western portion of Poland to Germany and the Eastern part to the Soviet Union.

In June of 1941 Germany unilaterally abrogated that non-aggression treaty with Stalin and launched a surprise attack against the Soviet Union. In their retreat the Soviets offered transportation to those who wished to escape the German invasion.

Some of those families that left Poland spent the war years in Siberia, others were resettled in Uzbekistan or Kazakhstan, southern states that were part of the Soviet Union. There is no question about the fact that the resettled Jews suffered great hardships. Their life must have been harsh in Siberia, but compared to what the Germans did to them in Poland, the Soviets saved the lives of many thousands of Jews.

After the war many of those families wished to return to their homes: to the towns and villages in Poland. Much to their surprise on their return they were not welcomed, in fact they were physically threatened and their lives were in danger. Once again, they became refugees and found safety in D.P. camps, in the hope that they would find a welcoming country to go to. Many of those families eventually landed in Israel, the United States, or Canada, some went to Australia.

In this DP camp I had the opportunity to meet people from different national backgrounds; Zionist organizations of every persuasion, from the ultra orthodox religious groups to the agnostics.

I was conflicted, I called into question both extremes, I was not alone, and there were others like myself with misgivings. I knew I could no longer be the obedient religious boy I had been brought up to be.

Without work or study, we had a lot of time to discuss and debate life and death issues, to the extent of our understanding. I participated in sports.

I became a member of our soccer team; we played against teams from other D.P. camps. I also played Ping-Pong (table tennis) a sport I was good at and liked very much.

I regret that I did not take advantage of that free time to read books and further my education. I fondly recall these other friends Joe Koopfersmith who picked snails off leaves of grass to survive in Ebensee concentration camp; a fine jeweler by trade. He designed and made beautiful jewelry. Mike Jucowics, who after liberation spent a year in a sanatorium for TB; fortunately he was cured. Mike's sister Bella and her husband W. Sevemy and of course Simon and Sidy, Herman and Luba, Freuka, the former partisan, Staig Joska a great Ping-Pong player, Zigany and Sam Moskowitch, the newly wed couple the Rosenbaums, Jancsi Kohn and many other friends whose names I can't recall, but I'll never forget their true friendship.

Janos Kohn (Jancsi) and his older brother Micklos (Mickey) shared an attic room. Mickey then married Joe Koopfersmith's aunt. Since there was a housing shortage, Jancsi had to find a roommate, before one was imposed on him, I moved in with him. Herman and Simon would never have suggested I leave, although the room we shared was so overcrowded. It was good for them and for me that I moved out. Jancsi and I turned out to become very compatible.

Jancsi Kohn grew up in a town near Budapest and spent six months in Bergen Belzen KZ camp. I think the community he comes from was also part of the Budapest Jews that the notorious Adolf Eichmann negotiated, promised to release in exchange for trucks. That infamous negotiation is well documented. Jews of Budapest were also deported but several months later, not in May off 1944. He and his three brothers survived, but the Nazis killed their parents.

We became very good friends; since he spoke only Hungarian I had an excellent opportunity to practice the language.

In most of the DP camps, large or small, there were Zionist groups active in recruiting future Zionists. They planned for the time they would be able to go to Palestine and hoped that day would come soon. I did not participate in their activities but I had great respect and admiration for those who did. Jancsi also took part in those meetings; from him I learned much about their activities.

There was not an ounce of Zionist conviction in him, his cause was special and personal. His reason for wanting to go to Palestine and fight for Israel's independence if necessary, was his brother. He was committed to finish the journey that his younger brother Shany could not. Shany was on a ship bound for Palestine that the British Navy prevented from landing. The ship was forced to disembark on the Island of Cyprus. The passengers were interned there for the duration and were treated no better than in German concentration camps. Shanyi became very sick and died shortly after he was allowed to land in Palestine. He was buried in Atlit, a small old town near the coastal city of Haifa.

I had other plans, I wanted to go to America. My roommate understood, he read my aunt's letters. Since I didn't understand English my aunt corresponded in Hungarian. My aunt tried everything to expedite my emigration, but the U.S. Immigration office was not to be rushed, I had to wait for my turn.

Peer pressure was hard to resist in camp, and the next year and a half was most difficult for me. Hundreds of young men and women, many close friends including my roommate, were ready to go to Palestine, and many left. At times I was at a breaking point, were it not for Jancsi, who always gave me moral support, I could not have stayed the course I chose for myself.

In 1947, about a month before Passover, I received a letter from Chaplain William Dalin, with an invitation to visit him on a certain date in Frankfurt. I had no idea what the invitation was about until my aunt informed me about this prearranged visit. I was excited about going to Frankfurt and maybe visit with my friends at the O.R.T. trade school in Offenbach, near Frankfurt, a city well known for its leather tanneries and fine leather products.

The day before my meeting with the Chaplain I took a train that was scheduled to arrive in Frankfurt about half-past-two in the morning. My appointment with Chaplain Dalin was for 10 am. Instead of staying at the train station I decided to go to Offenbach to visit my friends, and to freshen up for my appointment. The local train ride from Frankfurt to Offenbach was short and I had no difficulty finding the O.R.T. School. Since it was so very early I decided to rest until morning in one of the empty bunk beds in their dormitory. I overslept, when I woke up the room was very quiet, all had gone to their classes. I got dressed, my shoes were there, but my socks were not, they probably had been swept away. I rushed out in my sockless shoes, missed seeing my friends, and rushed to take the commuter train back to Frankfurt.

The former I. G. Farben Industries office complex (The DuPont of wartime Nazi Germany) was now the headquarters of the Allied powers in Europe. That was the address where I was to meet the Chaplain. It rained all morning, and I had no overcoat or hat so by the time I arrived at the gate I was completely drenched. I showed my invitation to the M. P. guards, my identity and invitation was checked, and then with an escort of four M.P.'s, I was promptly walked to the building and the office where I was to meet the Chaplain.

From the gate house our long walk took us past buildings that showed the flags of the victorious Allies. The building we entered, with its long marble corridors, was magnificent. The M.P.'s were polite, I was very impressed with the protocol, I looked like a street vagabond but they treated me kindly. They stopped in front of an office, one entered to announce my arrival.

The office was huge, with desks at opposite ends of the room. Even though it was still raining hard, daylight through the large windows made the room bright. As I entered I noticed an elegantly dressed, gray-haired woman sitting in a chair by the window reading a book.

She greeted me. When she realized I did not understand English she spoke to me in Yiddish. Evidently she knew I was coming and told me I had to wait, she said the Chaplain and her husband were in conference with the General next door. While we conversed she could not help but notice how shabby I looked. She excused herself and walked to a closet, brought out a shirt, socks and a beautiful black alpaca overcoat. She made me go to the bathroom and change into my new shirt and socks. I tried on the overcoat, it fit me well. It was one of her husband's coats. We talked for a while, she was interested in my background, where I came from, and about my future plans. She was a kind person.

Her husband Judge Lewis E. Levinthal of Philadelphia, was an official advisor to General Lucius Clay on Jewish affairs in Europe; the then Commander of the American military forces in Germany. By the time the Chaplain came into the room I was completely at ease. Shortly after we greeted each other, he handed me an envelope with a letter from my aunt.

The Chaplain's wife Bella, was from Brooklyn N.Y. She was the daughter of a family in my aunt's neighborhood. Bella Dalin was an officer of the American Joint Distribution Committee in Frankfurt. In her letter my aunt wrote that I should be patient, not to despair, and someday soon we'd be together. The letter also contained a 20 dollar bill. She always wrote how much she loved me. My aunt was like a mother to me. Before I left, the Chaplain invited me to the Passover Seder that would take place in Wiesbaden, and promised to mail me a written invitation. I felt like a new person. I was assured again that there were people who cared about me, and that I was not alone. There were thousands of stateless and homeless people all over post war Europe who could not be certain that they mattered and were not forgotten.

The Zionist groups had to operate in secrecy. Under the British, the doors to Palestine were closed and ships with Jewish refugees were not allowed to land.

Some were escorted to Cyprus, and the passengers were interned there into camps surrounded with barbed wire, a scary sight for survivors of Nazi concentration camps. The best known ship of that time was the "Exodus" it also was denied landing and was returned to the port of departure and its passengers detained.

Chaplain Dalin with headquarters in Wiesbaden was the head Chaplain for all the Jewish men serving in the U.S. Air Force in Europe. On my return to Wiesbaden a few weeks later I went straight to his office. He welcomed me and was very interested in knowing of how we spent our time in DP camp. He was glad to see me as a guest to the Passover Seder. The Chaplain described his function as chaplain to the Jewish men in the armed forces, in the US Air Force in particular, and to a special project, the restoration of the Jewish community center and synagogue of Wiesbaden. He arranged for me to stay with a local family for the holiday, he treated me to a bottle of Coca-Cola from a vending machine. That was the first Coke I ever had, it was in the original small pinched bottle.

During the Nazi years the Jewish community of Wiesbaden as in other German cities, was obliterated. Chaplain Dalin had a special interest in helping the community rebuild its synagogue and Jewish life. The Seder was held at the newly restored community center; hundreds of soldiers, airmen, private citizens and guests Chaplains of other faiths attended. It was a beautiful and joyful celebration.

Back in D.P. camp I was absorbed in sports, I listened to the radio and went to the movies with friends. There were few books to read. With so many different spoken languages it would have been close to impossible to organize a library. Correspondence with my aunt was regular. She informed me about the slow progress in acquiring the necessary documents she had to submit to the U.S. Immigration office. There were thousands of applicants, each had to wait for his or her turn. Priorities were given to applicants of families with small children.

Every month the D. P. camp's population became smaller. My roommate Jancsi left for Palestine, others moved to other D.P. camps.

I followed the events in Palestine. In late November 1947 the United Nations accepted the partition of Palestine into two states, one for the Jews and one for the Palestinians. In May 1948 the birth of the State of Israel became a fact. The Arabs refused to accept the U. N. partition, the neighboring Arab armies attacked the new State from all sides. Israel had to be defended at all costs.

I worried about my many friends who had gone to Israel, especially my friend and roommate Jancsi. At this time he was already caught up in the War of Independence. In Windsheim as in other DP camps, many who had not volunteered before to go to Israel did so then. I followed those events with much anxiety, I could not help feeling as an outsider. I had many sleepless nights; I felt I let my people down. Emotionally I was exhausted; I feared I'd get up one morning, volunteer and join a group that went to Israel. I needed time to think rationally. There were others whose desire was to go to countries other than Israel. Many were waiting for visas to Canada, or to Australia. Herman and Simon Lowy and Joe Kupfersmith were also waiting for visas to America.

I was pulled in many directions. Zionism had its attractions; how could anyone argue about the need for a Jewish homeland. That was a common purpose we all had. I was young, I could still go to Israel from America if need be. I could not disappoint my aunt who was waiting for me with open arms. I looked forward to be with my aunt in America.

In a letter from my aunt I had news about my half sister Rozsi and her family. Life in Romania became unbearable for them, they feared the Communist government. When I last saw my sister in 1946, she was pregnant with Yehuda, who was born in December of that year.

They wanted to leave Romania. Just to get out, they left all their possessions, they left everything. In spring of 1948 in transit to Israel they had to stay in Vienna until Tova her baby girl was born. She was born on the 4Th. of July 1948. Now they were four, a year-and-a-half-old little boy and a newborn. As new immigrants in Israel they lived in a tent city in Ashkelon near Ashdod, a town on the coast of the Mediterranean Sea.

In due time I began to receive notices from the Immigration Office informing me of the ongoing process. I had appointments for interviews with the Immigration authorities. Eventually, nine months into 1949, everything was in order.

On September 10, I was to report to a transit camp at the port city of Bremerhaven. During the last few months I had spent all my money—I was penniless. My gold ring was the only thing I had of value. My friend Joe Kupfersmith made it for me in Windsheim; he designed it and fabricated the mold. I watched him melt the gold before he poured it into the cast. I didn't want to part with it but had no choice. I sold it at a fraction of its value.

The three years I spent in the Displaced Persons camp in Windsheim, seemed like a lifetime. Not that I was treated badly; the UNNRA organization provided all the basic needs to everyone. We all received food, shelter, medical care, recreation opportunities, without exception no one was neglected. We were in Germany and I wanted so much to leave Germany, I wished with all my being never to step on that cursed land again. I wrote to my aunt when the date of departure was certain. For the passage I was assigned to the troop transport ship named General McRae. I had never been on a ship before. I didn't know what to expect. The ship was small compared to a passenger ship; others told me. We were bedded into three-tier-berths.

Soon as we passed through the English Channel and headed for the Atlantic we met with heavy storms and very rough seas. Down below, between the pounding ocean and us there were only the skeletal steel walls. We had no cabins, the berth's hung from chains, hooked up to the exposed steel structure above. After two nights of swinging in every direction I found out what it meant to be seasick. The third night I looked for another place where I could spend the night and sleep, somewhere toward the middle of the ship, I found a spot under a spiral staircase, I spent a night there under a blanket. Almost everyone became seasick; at mealtime the mess hall was nearly empty. After that one restful night and all that good food, my appetite came back. The crossing of the Atlantic was exciting. Winds from the North were so powerful; for more than a day the exits to the deck on that side were locked down.

Our troop transport ship was not large, the ocean waves tossed it in all directions. We were told that the month of September was not the best time for crossing the Atlantic. All the passengers were divided into work groups. We provided most of the maintenance, from scrubbing the decks to painting whatever needed painting on that ship. On the last days the weather improved and we all enjoyed the sea air and the meals. I was always amazed and overwhelmed by the great variety on the menu. Roasted turkey meat with cranberry sauce (a combination not known that time in Europe) and mashed potatoes with ketchup; that I liked best. We were introduced to ketchup in DP camp, a condiment unknown to me, I grew up without Ketchup. For breakfast we had all kinds of fruit juices, ham and eggs with bacon, fresh fruits, coffee; food was plentiful.

I remember that last night before landing. So many things to think about. The few days I spent on that small ship was not enough time to sort things out. Some of my friends, the Lowy brothers and others have left for America a few months before me, and others I left behind, they would come later. I missed being with, and among familiar faces. I really would have liked to have been with someone I could have shared memories, reflecting on past-unfulfilled wants and desires.

I was at the edge of beginning a new life in a new land. I was hopefully aware of the many thousands who had come before me.

I was not naive; I knew I may never want to go back to Europe, or to Romania in particular. I was anxious about meeting my aunt and uncle. Without them, their encouragement and financial help, I probably would have stayed in my home town in Bistrita, Romania. I was glad that I left when I did.

I was not a child anymore. I've been on my own since 1945, since liberation. Although I could speak several languages; Romanian, Hungarian, German, I had taken French and Latin in high school also, I had no wish to remain in Europe. I worried much too much about everything. I was grateful to the Americans who saved my life at Ebensee; they made it possible for me to live and then allow me to come and begin a new life in America. Then I realized the common thread that bound us on that ship; to begin anew in this land.

From past midnight, looking for approaching land, we stood five and six deep at the ship's rails. The night was dark and moonless. Out of the darkness, as far as the eye could see, an endless string of bright lights, the coastline of America, New York City began to show. As the horizon came closer, the darkness slowly turned to dawn. In the early predawn hours the troop transport ship "The General McCrae" lowered its anchors in the bay of NY. Its cargo, new immigrants, grateful Holocaust survivors.

After three years in DP camps in West Germany, I was allowed to emigrate to America. In the distance the flaming torch of the Statue of Liberty became more visible by the minute. The immigration officials came on board; after they examined our documents we were allowed to disembark.

My aunt, Mrs. Rose Hirsch, this wonderful loving aunt, was waiting for me. There I stood in front of the most important person in my life. She was like a mother to me.

After four years and so many delays, at times I wondered if I'll ever reach America; would that day ever come?

Her letters, her kindness, her genuine love and caring . . . I had so much, I was so lucky. I had so much more waiting for me than many others, for whom no one was waiting.

We embraced, in our joy she cried I cried with her it was a very happy moment for us; we shed tears freely. My aunt introduced me to Mrs. Goldstein her long time friend, who came with her to the dock. Then she said: "And now Shimi, we are going home to Brooklyn, your uncle is waiting for us."

On September 28, 1949 I began my new life in America. My luggage was a shiny aluminum valise, empty of possessions, but full of dreams. After all these years I still have the aluminum valise—I can't part with it.

DP Camp 1947. Me with Yuncsi—roomate

DP Camp 1947 Me & Simon

Chaplian Dalin Conducting Sedar in Wiesbaden 1947

DP Camp 1947 Football team

DP Camp. Team on wall 1947-48

Me in Bremerhaven 1949

USAT GENERAL J.H. McRAE
Office of the Transport Commander

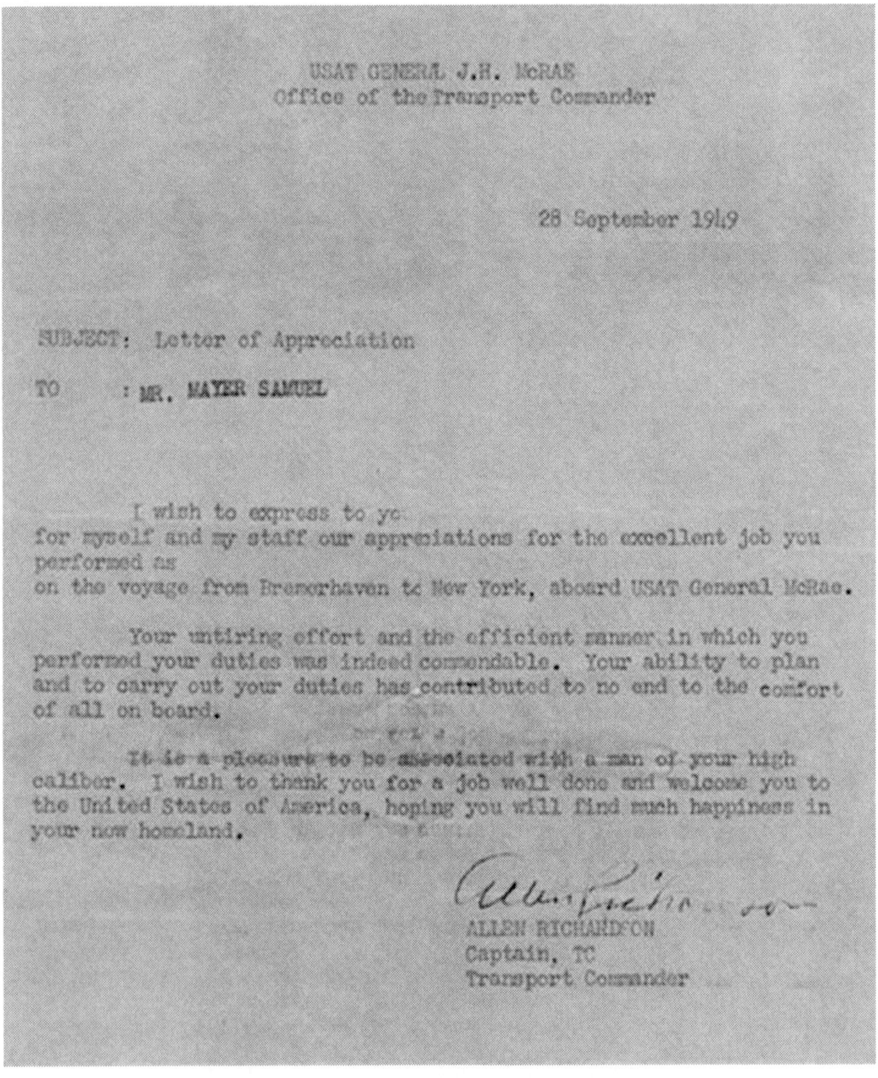

28 September 1949

SUBJECT: Letter of Appreciation

TO : MR. MAYER SAMUEL

I wish to express to yo
for myself and my staff our appreciations for the excellent job you performed as
on the voyage from Bremerhaven to New York, aboard USAT General McRae.

Your untiring effort and the efficient manner in which you performed your duties was indeed commendable. Your ability to plan and to carry out your duties has contributed to no end to the comfort of all on board.

It is a pleasure to be associated with a man of your high caliber. I wish to thank you for a job well done and welcome you to the United States of America, hoping you will find much happiness in your new homeland.

ALLEN RICHARDSON
Captain, TC
Transport Commander

Letter from the Captain of the USAT General McRae.
This is the ship that brought me to the United States

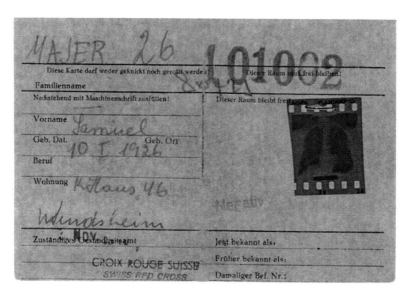

Health Card. Issued at DP camp.
Without it, I would not have been able to enter the United States

My Aunt & Uncle—Brooklyn NY

Postscript

In all the countries the Nazis occupied they turned normal life upside down. They brought destruction and misery, they turned neighbor against neighbor; in a few years they conquered both weak and stronger nations. The so called master race, their slogan "Deutschland Uber Alles", almost succeeded in killing all the Jews and enslaving the rest of the world.

Much has been written about what could or should have been done. Some say that those in power in the US and Britain including the Vatican in Rome, could have done more to help stop the Killings. The facts of that period are clouded by claims and counter claims.

President Roosevelt condemned the Nazi atrocities and promised that

"None Who Participated Would Go Unpunished"

It's naive to believe that every Nazi criminal, every murderer was caught tried and convicted after the war. Sadly some of those murderers are still walking among us.

Sixty plus years have passed since the end of World War II, while the survivors are dying out, the deniers of the Holocaust are growing in numbers. They are hard at work creating an environment; planting seeds of hatred against minorities, religions, and philosophies they disagree with.

All who are old enough to have witnessed the tragedies during the Nazi era, and before our stories fade from human memory we must inform and educate this generation, our future is in their hands. If we fail we may not be able to prevent it from happening again. A catastrophe not caused by an act of God or nature, but caused by evil people who had no regard for human life and dignity.

We must not forget what happened there.

Tomorrow's leaders will have to be accountable, more responsive to human needs. With instant communication we have the technological capacity to be informed of human catastrophes natural or man made in an instant. Metaphorically we may be able to hear a tree fall in the most distant forest.

CPSIA information can be obtained at www.ICGtesting.com
Printed in the USA
BVOW071132030313

314541BV00001B/88/P